THE STORY OF ATLANTIS

A GEOGRAPHICAL, HISTORICAL, AND ETHNOLOGICAL SKETCH.
ILLUSTRATED BY FOUR MAPS.

W. Scott-Elliot

Elefante Books

MMXXII

Copyright © 2022 Elefante Books

All rights reserved

No part of this book may be reproduced, stored in a retrieval system, or transmitted in any form or by any means, electronic, photocopying, recording, or otherwise, without the express permission of the publisher.

ISBN 9798360449287

Content

Preface iii
The Story of Atlantis 11
MAPS 123

Preface

For readers unacquainted with the progress made in recent years by earnest students of occultism attached to the Theosophical Society, the significance of the statement embodied in the following pages would be misapprehended without the significance of the statement embodied in following pages some preliminary explanation. Historical research has depended for western civilization hitherto, on written records of one kind or another. When literary memoranda have fallen short, stone monuments have sometimes been available, and fossil remains have given us a few unequivocal, though inarticulate assurances concerning the antiquity of humans; but modern culture has lost sight of or has overlooked possibilities connected with the investigation of past events, which are independent of fallible evidence transmitted to us by ancient writers. The world at large is thus at present so imperfectly alive to the resources of human faculty, that by most people as yet, the very existence, even as a potentiality, of psychic powers, which some of us all the while are consciously exercising every day, is scornfully denied and derided. The situation is sadly ludicrous from the point of view of those who appreciate the prospects of evolution because mankind is thus willfully holding at arm's length, the knowledge that is essential to its own ulterior progress. The maximum cultivation of which the human intellect is susceptible while it denies itself all the resources of its higher spiritual consciousness can never be more than a preparatory process as compared with that which may set in when the faculties are sufficiently enlarged to enter into a conscious relationship with the super-physical planes or aspects of Nature.

For anyone who will have the patience to study the published results of psychic investigation over the last fifty years, the reality of clairvoyance as an occasional phenomenon of human intelligence must establish itself on an immovable foundation. For those who, without being occultists— students that are to say of Nature's loftier aspects, in a position to obtain better teaching than that which any written books can give— for those who merely avail themselves of recorded evidence, a declaration on the part of others of disbelief in the possibility of clairvoyance, is on a level with the proverbial African's disbelief in ice. But the experiences of clairvoyance that have accumulated in the hands of those who have studied it in connection with mesmerism, do no more than prove the existence in human nature of a capacity for cognizing physical phenomena distant either in space or time, in some way which has nothing to do with the physical senses. Those who have studied the mysteries of clairvoyance in connection with theosophic teaching have been enabled to realize that the ultimate resources of that faculty range as far beyond its humbler manifestations, dealt with by unassisted enquirers, as the resources of the higher mathematics exceed those of the abacus. Clairvoyance, indeed, is of many kinds, all of which fall easily into their places when we appreciate the manner in which human consciousness functions on different planes of Nature. The faculty of reading the pages of a closed book, or of discerning objects blindfolded, or at a distance from the observer, is quite a different faculty from that employed on the cognition of past events. That last is the kind of which it is necessary to say something here, in order that the true character of the present treatise on Atlantis may be understood, but I allude to the others merely that the explanation I have to give may not be mistaken for a complete theory of clairvoyance in all its varieties.

We may best be helped to comprehension of clairvoyance as related to past events, by considering in the first instance the phenomena of memory. The theory of memory which relates it to an imaginary rearrangement of physical molecules of brain matter, going on at every instant of our lives, is one that presents itself as plausible to no one who can ascend one degree above the thinking level of the uncompromising atheistically materialist. To everyone who accepts, as even a reasonable hypothesis, the idea that a man is something more than a crease in a state of animation, it must be a reasonable hypothesis that memory has to do with that principle in man which is super-physical. His memory in short, is a function of some other than the physical plane. The pictures of memory are imprinted, it is clear, on some nonphysical medium, and are accessible to the embodied thinker in ordinary cases by virtue of some effort he makes in as to exercise the faculty of astral clairvoyance. That term may be conveniently used to denote the kind of clairvoyance I am now endeavoring to elucidate, the kind which, in some of its more magnificent developments, has been employed to carry out the investigations on the basis of which the present account of Atlantis has been compiled.

There is no limit really to the resources of astral clairvoyance in investigations concerning the past history of the earth, whether we are concerned with the events that have befallen the human race in pre-historic epochs, or with the growth of the planet itself through geological periods which antedated the advent of man, or with more recent events, current narrations of which have been distorted by careless or perverse historians. The memory of Nature is infallibly accurate and inexhaustibly minute. A time will come as certainly as the precession of the equinoxes, when the literary method of historical research will be laid aside as out of date, in the case of all original work. People among us who are capable of exercising astral clairvoyance in full perfection— but have not yet been called away to higher functions in connection with the promotion of human progress, of which ordinary humanity at present knows even less than an Indian ryot knows of cabinet councils— are still very few. Those who know what the few can do, and through what processes of training and self-discipline they have passed in pursuit of interior ideas, of which when attained astral clairvoyance is but an individual circum- stance, are many, but still a small minority as compared with the modem cultivated world. But as time goes on, and within a measurable future, some of us have reason to feel sure that the numbers of those who are competent to exercise astral clairvoyance will increase sufficiently to extend the circle of those who are aware of their capacities, till it comes to embrace all the intelligence and culture of civilized mankind only a few generations hence. Meanwhile, the present volume is the first that has been put forward as the pioneer essay of the new method of historical research. It is amusing to all who are concerned with it, to think how inevitably it will be mistaken— for some little while as yet, by materialistic readers, unable to accept the frank explanation here given of the principle on which it has been prepared— for a work of imagination.

For the benefit of others who may be more intuitive it may be well to say a word or two that may guard them from supposing that because historical research by means of astral clairvoyance is not impeded by having to deal with periods removed from our own by hundreds of thousands of years, it is on that account a process which involves no trouble. Every fact stated in the present volume has been picked up bit by bit with watchful and attentive care, in the course of an investigation on which more than one qualified person has been engaged, in the intervals of other activity, for some years past. And to promote the success of their work they have been allowed access to some maps and other records physically preserved from the remote periods concerned— though in safer keeping than in that of the turbulent races occupied in Europe with the development of civilization in brief intervals of leisure from warfare, and hard pressed by the fanaticism that so long treated science as sacrilegious during the Middle Ages of Europe.

Laborious as the task has been, however, it will be recognized as amply repaying the trouble taken, by everyone who is able to perceive how absolutely necessary to a proper comprehension of the world as we find it, is a proper comprehension of its preceding Atlantean phase. Without this knowledge, all speculations concerning ethnology are futile and misleading. The course of race development is chaos and confusion without the key furnished by the character of Atlantean civilization and the configuration of the earth at the Atlantean periods. Geologists know that land and ocean surfaces must have repeatedly changed places during the period at which they also know— from the situation of human remains in the various strata— that the lands were inhabited. And yet for want of accurate knowledge as to the dates at which the changes took place, they discard the whole theory from their practical thinking, and except for certain hypotheses started by naturalists dealing with the southern hemisphere, have generally endeavored to harmonize race migrations with the configuration of the earth in existence at the present time.

In this way nonsense is made of the whole retrospect; and the ethnological scheme remains so vague and shadowy that it fails to displace crude conceptions of mankind's beginning which still dominate religious thinking and keep back the spiritual progress of the age. The decadence and ultimate disappearance of Atlantean civilization is in turn as instructive as its rise and glory; but I have now accomplished the main purpose with which I sought leave to introduce the work now before the world, with a brief prefatory explanation, and if its contents fail to convey a sense of its importance to any listeners I am now addressing, that result could hardly be accomplished by further recommendations of mine.

A.P. SINNETT

The Story of Atlantis

The general scope of the subject before us will best be realized by considering the amount of information that is obtainable about the various nations that compose our great fifth or Aryan Race.

From the time of the Greeks and the Romans onwards volumes have been written about every people who in their turn have filled the stage of history. The political institutions, the religious beliefs, the social and domestic manners, and customs have all been analyzed and cataloged, and countless works in many tongues record for our benefit the march of progress.

Further, it must be remembered that of the history of this fifth Race we possess but a fragment— the record merely of the last family races of the Keltic sub-race, and the first family races of our own Teutonic stock.

But the hundreds of thousands of years that elapsed from the time when the earliest Aryans left their home on the shores of the central Asian Sea to the time of the Greeks and Romans, bore witness to the rise and fall of innumerable civilizations. Of the first sub-race of our Aryan Race who inhabited India and colonized Egypt in prehistoric times we know practically nothing, and the same may be said of the Chaldean, Babylonian, and Assyrian nations who composed the 2nd sub-race— for the fragments of knowledge obtained from the recently deciphered hieroglyphs or cuneiform inscriptions on Egyptian tombs or Babylonian tablets can scarcely be said to constitute history. The Persians who belonged to the 3rd or Iranian sub-race have it is true, left a few more traces, but of the earlier civilizations of the Celtic or 4th sub-race, we have no records at all. It is only with the rise of the last family shoots of this Celtic stock, viz., the Greek and Roman peoples, that we come upon historical times.

In addition, also to the blank period in the past, there is a blank period in the future. Of the seven sub-races required to complete the history of a great Root Race, five only have so far come into existence. Our own Teutonic or 5th sub-race has already developed many nations but has not yet run its course, while the 6th and 7th sub-races, who will be developed on the continents of North and South America, will have thousands of years of history to give to the world.

In attempting, therefore, to summarize in a few pages' information about the world's progress during a period which must have occupied at least as great a stretch of years as that above referred to, it must be realized how slight a sketch this must inevitably be.

A record of the world's progress during the period of the Fourth or Atlantean Race must embrace the history of many nations and register the rise and fall of many civilizations. Catastrophes, too, on a scale such as have not yet been experienced during the life of our present Fifth Race, took place on more than one occasion during the progress of the Fourth. The destruction of Atlantis was accomplished by a series of catastrophes varying in character from great cataclysms in which whole territories and populations perished, to comparatively unimportant landslips such as occur on our own coasts today. When the destruction was once inaugurated by the first great catastrophe there was no intermission of the minor landslips which continued slowly but steadily to eat away the continent. Four of the great catastrophes stand out above the rest in magnitude. The first took place in the Miocene age, about 800,000 years ago. The second, which was of minor importance, occurred about 200,000 years ago. The third— about 80,000 years ago— was a very great one. It destroyed all that remained of the Atlantean continent, with the exception of the island to which Plato gave the name of Poseidonis, which in its turn was submerged in the fourth and final great catastrophe of 9,564 b. c.

Now the testimony of the oldest writers and of modern scientific research alike bear witness to the existence of an ancient continent occupying the site of the lost Atlantis. Before proceeding to the consideration of the subject itself, it is proposed cursorily to glance at the generally known sources which supply corroborative evidence. These may be grouped into the five following classes:

First, the testimony of the deep-sea soundings.

Second, the distribution of fauna and flora.

Third, the similarity of language and of ethnological type.

Fourth, the similarity of religious belief, ritual, and architecture.

Fifth, the testimony of ancient writers, of early race traditions, and of archaic flood legends.

In the first place, then, the testimony of the deep-sea soundings may be summarized in a few words. Thanks chiefly to the expeditions of the British and American gunboats, "Challenger" and "Dolphin" (though Germany also was associated with this scientific exploration) the bed of the whole Atlantic Ocean is now mapped out, with the result that an immense bank or ridge of great elevation is shown to exist in mid-Atlantic. This ridge stretches in a south-westerly direction from about fifty degrees north towards the coast of South America, then in a south-easterly direction towards the coast of Africa, changing its direction again about Ascension Island, and running due south to Tristan D'Cunha. The ridge rises almost sheer about 9,000 feet from the ocean depths around it, while the Azores, St. Paul, Ascension, and Tristan D'Cunha are the peaks of this land that still remain above water. A line of 3,500 fathoms, or say, 21,000 feet, is required to sound the deepest parts of the Atlantic, but the higher parts of the ridge are only a hundred to a few hundred fathoms beneath the sea.

The soundings too showed that the ridge is covered with volcanic debris of which traces are to be found right across the ocean to the American coasts. Indeed, the fact that the ocean bed, particularly about the Azores, has been the scene of volcanic disturbance on a gigantic scale, and that within a quite measurable period of geologic time, is conclusively proved by the investigations made during the above-named expeditions.

Mr. Starkie Gardner is of opinion that in the Eocene times the British Islands formed part of a larger island or continent stretching into the Atlantic, and "that a great tract of land formerly existed where the sea now is, and that Cornwall, the Scilly, and the Channel Islands, Ireland and Brittany are the remains of its highest summits" (*Pop. Sc. Review, July 1878*).

Second. —The proven existence on continents separated by great oceans of similar or identical species of fauna and flora is a standing puzzle to biologists and botanists alike. But if a link between these continents once existed allowing for the natural migration of such animals and plants, the puzzle is solved. Now the fossil remains of the camel are found in India, Africa, South America, and Kansas: but it is one of the generally accepted hypotheses of naturalists that every species of animal and plant originated in but one part of the globe, from which center it gradually overran the other portions. How then can the fact of such fossil remains be accounted for without the existence of land communication in some remote age? Recent discoveries in the fossil beds of Nebraska seem also to prove that the horse originated in the Western Hemisphere, for that is the only part of the world where fossil remains have been discovered, showing the various intermediate forms which have been identified as the precursors of the true horse. It would therefore be difficult to account for the presence of the horse in Europe except on the hypothesis of continuous land communication between the two continents, seeing that it is certain that the horse existed in a wild state in Europe and Asia before his domestication by man, which may be traced back almost to the stone age. Cattle and sheep as we now know them to have an equally remote ancestry. Darwin finds domesticated cattle in Europe in the earliest part of the stone age, having long before developed out of wild forms akin to the buffalo of America. Remains of the cave lion of Europe are also found in North America.

Turning now from the animal to the vegetable kingdom it appears that the greater part of the flora of the Miocene age in Europe— found chiefly in the fossil beds of Switzerland— exist in the present day in America, some of them in Africa. But the noteworthy fact about America is that while the greater proportion is to be found in the Eastern

States, very many are wanting on the Pacific coast. This seems to show that it was from the Atlantic side that they entered the continent. Professor Asa Gray says that out of 66 genera and 155 species found in the forest east of the Rocky Mountains, only 31 genera and 78 species are found west of these heights. But the greatest problem of all is the plantain or banana. Professor Kuntze, an eminent Germán botanist, asks, "In what way was this plant" (a native of tropical Asia and Africa) "which cannot stand a voyage through the temperate zone, carried to America?" As he points out, the plant is seedless, it cannot be propagated by cuttings, and neither has it a tuber that could be easily transported. Its root is tree-like. To transport it special care would be required, nor could it stand a long transit. The only way in which he can account for its appearance in America is to suppose that it must have been transported by the civilized man at a time when the polar regions had a tropical climate! He adds, 11 a cultivated plant which does not possess seeds must have been under culture for a very long period... it is perhaps fair to infer that these plants were cultivated as early as the beginning of the Diluvial period." Why it may be asked, should not this inference take us back to still earlier times, and where did the civilization necessary for the plant's

The Story of Atlantis

cultivation exist, or the climate and circumstances requisite for its transportation, unless there were at some time a link between the old world and the new? Professor Wallace in his delightful Island Life as well as other writers in many important works have put forward ingenious hypotheses to account for the identity of flora and fauna on widely separated lands, and for their transit across the ocean, but all are unconvincing, and all break down at different points. It is well known that wheat as we know it has never existed in a truly wild state, nor is there any evidence tracing its descent from fossil species. Five varieties of wheat were already cultivated in Europe in the stone age— one variety found in the "Lake dwellings" being known as Egyptian wheat, from which Darwin argues that the Lake dwellers "either still kept up commercial intercourse with some southern people or had originally proceeded as colonists from the south." He concludes that wheat, barley, oats, etc., are descended from various species now extinct, or so widely different as to escape identification in which case he says: "Man must have cultivated cereals from an enormously remote period." 'The regions where these extinct species flourished, and the civilization under which they were cultivated by the intelligent selection, are both supplied by the lost continent whose colonists carried them east and west.

Third. —From the fauna and flora, we now turn to man.

Language. —The Basque language stands alone amongst European tongues, having an affinity with none of them. According to Farrar, "there never has been any doubt that this isolated language, preserving its identity in a western corner of Europe, between two mighty kingdoms, resembles in its structure the aboriginal languages of the vast opposite continent (América) and those alone" (Families of Speech, p. 132).

The Phoenicians apparently were the first nation in the Eastern Hemisphere to use a phonetic alphabet, the characters being regarded as mere signs for sounds. It is a curious fact that at an equally early date we find a phonetic alphabet in Central America amongst the Mayas of Yucatán, whose traditions ascribe the origin of their civilization to a land across the sea to the east. Le Plongeon[1], the

---

[1] Augustus Henry Julian Le Plongeon (May 4, 1825 – December 13, 1908) was a British-American archeologist and photographer who studied the pre-Columbian ruins of America, particularly those of the Maya civilization on the northern Yucatán Peninsula. While his writings contain many notions that were not well received by his contemporaries and were later disproven, Le Plongeon left a lasting legacy in his photographs documenting the ancient

great authority on this subject, writes: "One-third of this tongue (the Maya) is pure Greek. Who brought the dialect of Homer to America? or who took to Greece that of the Mayas? Greek is the offspring of the Sanskrit. Is Maya? or are they coeval?" Still more surprising is it to find thirteen letters out of the Maya alphabet bearing most distinct relation to the Egyptian hieroglyphic signs for the same letters. It is probable that the earliest form of alphabet was hieroglyphic, "the writing of the Gods," as the Egyptians called it, and that it developed later in Atlantis into the phonetic. It would be natural to assume that the Egyptians were an early colony from Atlantis (as they actually were)

---

ruins. He was one of the earliest proponents of Mayanism. By the 1880s, while most Mayanists accepted that the Maya civilization postdated Ancient Egypt, Le Plongeon stood by his theories. He cited his years of fieldwork and studies of archival sources and challenged those he considered "armchair" archaeologists to debate the issues. However, as evidence mounted against cultural diffusion, Le Plongeon became marginalized, and his theories fell further outside the growing mainstream of Maya archaeology. Le Plongeon insisted that the symbols of Freemasonry could be traced to the ancient Maya and that the ancient knowledge had come to ancient Egypt from the ancient Maya by way of Atlantis. He and Alice constructed an imaginative "history" with the Maya sites in Yucatán being the cradle of civilization, with civilization then traveling east first to Atlantis and later to Ancient Egypt. The Le Plongeons named kings and queens of these dynasties and said that various artworks were portraits of such ancient royalty (such as the famous Chacmool, which the couple excavated at Chichén Itzá). The Le Plongeons reconstructed a detailed but fanciful story of Queen Moo and Prince Coh (also known as "Chac Mool") in which Prince Coh's death resulted in the erection of monuments in his honor (similar to the commemoration of Prince Albert by Queen Victoria) (N. of E.)

and that they carried away with them the primitive type of writing which has thus left its traces on both hemispheres, while the Phoenicians, who were asea-going people, obtained and assimilated the later form of alphabet during their trading voyages with the people of the west.

One more point may be noticed, m., the extraordinary re- semblance between many words in the Hebrew language and words bearing precisely the same meaning in the tongue of the Chiapanecas— a branch of the Maya race, and amongst the most ancient in Central América. A list of these words is given in North Americans of Antiquity, p. 475.

The similarity of language among the various savage's races of the Pacific islands has been used as an argument by writers on this subject. The existence of similar languages among races separated by leagues of ocean, across which in history time they are known to have had no means of transport, is certainly an argument in favor of their descent from a single race occupying a single continent, but the argument cannot be used here, for the continent in question was not Atlantis, but the still earlier Lemuria.

Ethnological Types. —Atlantis as we shall see is said to have been inhabited by red, yellow, white, and black races. It is now proved by the research of Le Plongeon, De Quatrefages[2], Bancroft[3], and others that black populations of negroid type existed even up to recent times in America. Many of the monuments of Central America are decorated with negro faces, and some of the idols found there are clearly intended to represent negros, with small skulls, short woolly hair, and thick lips. The Popul Vuh, speaking of the first home of the Guatemalan race, says that "black and white men together" lived

---

[2] Jean Louis Armand de Quatrefages de Bréau (10 February 1810 – 12 January 1892) was a French biologist. Quatrefages was critical of Charles Darwin's theories but was not anti-evolution. From 1859 he corresponded with Darwin regularly and although they disagreed with each other they stayed on friendly terms. Quatrefages authored Charles Darwin et ses précurseurs francais (1870), which contained criticism of Darwinism. On receiving the book, Darwin in a letter to Quatrefages commented that "many of your strictures are severe enough, but all are given with perfect courtesy & fairness. I can truly say I would rather be criticized by you in this manner than praised by many others." In 1870, Quatrefages and Henri Milne-Edwards nominated Darwin for election as a corresponding member of the French Academy of Sciences in the section of Anatomy and Zoology. This was met with strong opposition from Émile Blanchard, Charles-Philippe Robin and others. Darwin lost the election by a narrow margin. In his book L'Espèce humaine (translated The Human Species, 1879) he disputed the role of natural selection in evolution. Quatrefages proposed that natural "elimination" would have been a more exact term as natural selection does not create new species. Quatrefages was a strict monogenist and was an opponent of polygenism)

[3] Hubert Howe Bancroft (May 5, 1832 – March 2, 1918) was an American historian and ethnologist who wrote, published and collected works concerning the western United States, Texas, California, Alaska, Mexico, Central America and British Columbia

in this happy land "in great peace," speaking "one language." (See Bancroft's Native Races, p. 547.) The Popul Vuh goes on to relate how the people migrated from their ancestral home, how their language became filtered, and how some went to the east, while others traveled west (to Central America).

Professor Retzius[4], in his Smithsonian Report, considers that the primitive dolichocephaly of America is nearly related to the Guanches of the Canary Islands, and to the population on the Atlantic seaboard of Africa, which Latham[5] comprises under the name of Egyptian-Atlantidae. The same form of the skull is found in the Canary Islands off the African coast and the Caribbean Islands off the American coast, while the color of the skin in both is of a reddish-brown.

The ancient Egyptians depicted themselves as red mien of much the same complexion as exists today among some tribes of American Indians. "The

---

[4] Anders Adolph Retzius (13 October 1796 – 18 April 1860), was a Swedish professor of anatomy and a supervisor at the Karolinska Institute in Stockholm.

[5] Robert Gordon Latham FRS (24 March 1812 – 9 March 1888) was an English ethnologist and philologist. Along with Prichard, however, Latham criticized Cuvier's use of the "Caucasian race" concept; and he preferred to avoid the term "race", preferring instead to "varieties of man", as a reaction to the rise of polygenist theory around 1850.

ancient Peruvians" says Short, "appear from numerous examples of hair found in their tombs to leave been an auburn-haired race."

A remarkable fact about the American Indians, and one which is a standing puzzle to ethnologists, is the wide range of color and complexion to be found among them. From the white tint of the Menominee, Dakota, Mandan, and Zuni tribes, many of whom have auburn hair and blue eyes, to the almost negro blackness of the Raros of Kansas and the now extinct tribes of California, the Indian races run through every shade of red-brown, copper, olive, cinnamon, and bronze (See and Short's North Americans of Antiquity[6], Winchell's pre-adamites[7] Catlin's Indians of North América / see also Atlantis, by Ignatius Donnelly[8] who has

---

[6] Short, John T. (John Thomas) (1850-1883).

[7] Alexander Winchell (December 31, 1824, in Northeast, New York – February 19, 1891, in Ann Arbor, Michigan) was a United States geologist who contributed to this field mainly as an educator and a popular lecturer and author. His views on evolution aroused controversy among his contemporaries. In 1875, he worked as a professor of geology and zoology at Vanderbilt University. There, his views on evolution, as expressed in his book Adamites and Preadamites: or, A Popular Discussion (1878), were not acceptable to the University administration because they diverged from Biblical teaching. He was much concerned with reconciling science and religion. He was an advocate of theistic evolution.

[8] Ignatius Loyola Donnelly (November 3, 1831 – January 1, 1901) was an American Congressman, populist writer, and fringe scientist. He is known primarily now for his fringe theories concerning Atlantis, Catastrophism (especially the idea of an ancient impact event affecting ancient civilizations),

collected a great mass of evidence under this and other heads) We shall see by and by how the diversity of complexion on the American continent is accounted for by the original race-tints on the parent continent of Atlantis.

Fourth. —Nothing seems to have surprised the first Spanish adventurers in México and Perú more than the extraordinary similarity to those of the old world, of the religious beliefs, rites, and emblems which they found established in the new. The Spanish priests regarded this similarity as the work of the devil.

The worship of the cross by the natives, and its constant presence in all religious buildings and ceremonies, was the principal subject of their amazement; and indeed nowhere— not even in India and Egypt— was this symbol held in more profound veneration than amongst the primitive tribes of the American continents, while the meaning underlying its worship was identical. In the west, as in the east, the cross was the symbol of life— sometimes of life physical, more often of life

---

and Shakespearean authorship, which many modern historians consider to be pseudoscience and pseudohistory. Donnelly's work corresponds to the writings of late-19th and early-20th century figures such as Helena Blavatsky, Rudolf Steiner, and James Churchward.

eternal.

In like manner in both hemispheres the worship of the sun disk or circle, and of the serpent, was universal, and more surprising still is the similarity of the word signifying "God" in the principal languages of east and west. Compare the Sanskrit "Dyaus" or "Dyaus-pitar," the Greek "Theos" and Zeus, the Latin "Deus" and "Jupiter," the Keltic "Dia" and "Ta" pronounced " Thyah " (seeming to bear affinity to the Egyptian Tau), the Jewish " Jah " or " Yah " and lastly the Mexican " Teo " or " Zeo".

Baptismal rites were practiced by all nations. In Babylon and Egypt, the candidates for initiation into the Mysteries were first baptized. Tertullian in his De Baptism says that they were promised in consequence "regeneration and the pardon of all their perjuries." The Scandinavian nations practiced baptism of new-born children; and when we turn to México and Perú we find infant baptism there as a solemn ceremonial, consisting of water sprinkling, the sign of the cross, and prayers for the washing away of sin (see Humboldt's Mexican Research and Prescott's México).

In addition to baptism, the tribes of México, Central America and Perú resembled the nations of the old world in their rites of confession, absolution, fasting, and marriage before priests by joining hands. They had even a ceremony resembling the Eucharist, in which cakes marked with the Tau (an Egyptian form of cross) were eaten, the people calling them the flesh of their God. These exactly resemble the sacred cakes of Egypt and other eastern nations. Like these nations too, the people of the new world had monastic orders, male and female, in which broken vows were punished with death. Like the Egyptians they embalmed their dead, they worshipped sun, moon, and planets, but over and above these adored a Deity "omnipresent, who knows all things .... invisible, incorporeal, one God of perfect perfection" (see Sahagun's Historia de Nueva España, lib. vi.).

They too had their virgin-mother goddess, "Our Lady" whose son, the "Lord of Light," was called the "Savior" bearing an accurate correspondence to Isis, Beltis, and the many other virgin goddesses of the east with their divine sons.

Their rites of sun and fire worship closely resembled those of the early Celts of Britain and Ireland, and like the latter they claimed to be the 11 children of the sun." An ark or argha was one of the universal sacred symbols which we find alike in India, Chaldea, Assyria, Egypt, Greece and among the Keltic peoples. Lord Kingsborough in his Mexican Antiquities (vol. viii. p. 250) says: "As among the Jews the ark was a sort of portable temple in which the deity was supposed to be continually present, so among the Mexicans, the Cherokees and the Indians of Michoacan and Honduras, an ark was held in the highest veneration and was considered an object too sacred to be touched by any but the priests."

As to religious architecture, we find on both sides of the Atlantic that one of the earliest sacred buildings is the pyramid. Doubtful as are the uses for which these structures were originally intended, one thing is clear, that they were closely connected with some religious idea or group of ideas. The identity of design in the pyramids of Egypt and those of México and Central América is too striking to be a mere coincidence.

True some— the greater number— of the American pyramids are of the truncated or flattened form, yet according to Bancroft and others, many of those found in Yucatán, and notably those near Palenque, are pointed at the top in true Egyptian fashion, while on the other hand, we have some of the

Egyptian pyramids of the stepped and flattened type. Cholula has been compared to the groups of Dachour, Sakkara, and the step pyramid of Medourn. Alike in orientation, in structure, and even in their internal galleries and chambers, these mysterious monuments of the east and of the west stand as witnesses to some common source whence their builders drew their plan.

The vast remains of cities and temples in México and Yucatán also strangely resemble those of Egypt, the ruins of Teotihuacan having frequently been compared to those of Karnak. The "false arch"— horizontal courses of stone, each slightly over-lapping the other— is found to be identical in Central America, in the oldest buildings of Greece, and in Etruscan remains. The mound builders of both eastern and western continents formed similar tumuli over their dead and laid the bodies in similar stone coffins. Both continents have their great serpent mounds; compare that of Adams Co., Ohio, with the fine serpent mound discovered in Argyleshire, or the less perfect specimen at Avebury in Wilts' The very carving and decoration of the temples of América, Egypt and India have much in common, while some of the mural decorations are absolutely identical.

Fifth. —It only remains now to summarize some of the evidence obtainable from ancient writers, from early race traditions, and from archaic flood-legends.

Aelian[9] in his *Varia Historia* (lib. iii. Ch. xviii.), states that Theopompus[10] (400 b. c.) recorded an interview between the King of Phrygia and Silenus, in which the latter referred to the existence of a great continent beyond the Atlantic, larger than Asia, Europe, and Libya together.

Proclus quotes an extract from an ancient writer who refers to the islands in the sea beyond the Pillars of Hercules (Straits of Gibraltar) and says that the inhabitants of one of these islands had a tradition from their ancestors of an extremely large island called Atlantis, which for a long time ruled over all the islands of the Atlantic Ocean.

---

[9] Claudius Aelianus (c. 175 – c. 235 AD), commonly Aelian born at Praeneste, was a Roman author and teacher of rhetoric who flourished under Septimius Severus and probably outlived Elagabalus, who died in 222. He spoke Greek so fluently that he was called "honey-tongued" (μελίγλωσσος meliglossos); Roman-born, he preferred Greek authors, and wrote in a slightly archaizing Greek himself. His two chief works are valuable for the numerous quotations from the works of earlier authors, which are otherwise lost, and for the surprising lore, which offers unexpected glimpses into the Greco-Roman world-view. It is also the only Greco-Roman work to mention Gilgamesh.
[10] Theopompus (Greek: Θεόπομπος, Theópompos; c. 380 BC – c. 315 BC) was an ancient Greek historian and rhetorician

Marcellus speaks of seven islands in the Atlantic, and states that their inhabitants preserve the memory of a much greater island, Atlantis, "which had for a long-time exercised dominion over the smaller ones."

Diodorus Siculus relates that the Phoenicians discovered "a large island in the Atlantic Ocean beyond the Pillars of Hercules several days' sail from the coast of Africa. "But the greatest authority on this subject is Plato. In the Timaeus he refers to the island continent, while the Critias or Atlanticus is nothing less than a detailed account of the history, arts, manners, and customs of the people. In the Timaeus he refers to "a mighty warlike power, rushing from the Atlantic Sea and spreading itself with hostile fury over all Europe and Asia. For at that time the Atlantic Sea was navigable and had an island before that mouth which is called by you the Pillars of Hercules. But this island was greater than both Libya and all Asia together, and afforded an easy passage to other neighboring islands, as it was likewise easy to pass from those islands to all the continents which border on this Atlantic Sea."

There is so much value in the Critias that it is not easy to choose, but the following extract is given, as it bears on the material resources of the country:

"They had likewise everything provided for them which both in a city and every other place is sought after as useful for the purposes of use. And they were supplied indeed with many things from foreign countries, on account of their extensive empire, but the island afforded them the greater part of everything of which they stood in need. In the first place the island supplied them with such things as are dug out of mines in a solid state, and with such as are melted: and orichalcum, which is now but seldom mentioned, but then was much celebrated, was dug out of the earth in many parts of the island and was considered as the most honorable of all metals except gold. Whatever, too, the woods afforded for builders the island produced in abundance. There were likewise sufficient pastures there for tame and savage animals, together with a prodigious number of elephants. For there were pastures for all such animals as are fed in lakes and rivers, on mountains and in plains. And in like manner there was sufficient aliment for the largest and most voracious kind of animals. Besides this, whatever of odoriferous the earth nourishes at present, whether roots, or grass, or wood, or juices, or gums, flowers, or fruits— these the island produced and produced them well."

The Gauls[11] possessed traditions of Atlantis which were collected by the Roman historian, Timagenes[12], who lived in the first century, b. c. Three distinct peoples apparently dwelt in Gaul. First, the indigenous population (probably the remains of a Lemurian race), second, the invaders from the distant island of Atlantis, and third, the Aryan Gauls (see pre-Adamites, p. 380).

The Toltecs of México traced themselves back to a starting- point called Atlan or Aztlan; the Aztecs also claimed to come from Aztlan (see Bancroft's Native Races, vol. v. pp. 221 and 321).

The Popul Vuh (p. 294) speaks of a visit paid by three sons of the Ring of the Quiches to a land "in the east on the shores of the sea whence their fathers had come" from which they brought back amongst other things "a system of writing" (see also

---

[11] Gauls were a group of Celtic peoples of mainland Europe in the Iron Age and the Roman period (roughly 5th century BC to 5th century AD). Their homeland was known as Gaul (Gallia). They spoke Gaulish, a continental Celtic language.

[12] Timagenes was a Greek writer, historian and teacher of rhetoric. He came from Alexandria, was captured by Romans in 55 BC and taken to Rome, where he was purchased by Faustus Cornelius Sulla, son of Sulla.[1] It is said that Timagenes had a falling-out with emperor Augustus, whereupon he destroyed his writings and fled Rome. He also asked Cleopatra to deliver Mark Antony to the Octavianus, or have him put to death. During his life Timagenes wrote a Universal History (until the time of Caesar) and a History of the Gauls.

Bancroft, vol. v. p. 553).

Amongst the Indians of North América there is a very general legend that their fore fathers came from a land "toward the sun-rising." The Iowa and Dakota Indians, according to Major J. Lind, believed that "all the tribes of Indians were formerly one and dwelt together on an island... towards the sunrise" They crossed the sea from thence "in huge Skiffs in which the Dakotas of old floated for weeks, finally gaining dry land."

The Central American books state that a part of the American continent extended far into the Atlantic Ocean and that this region was destroyed by a series of frightful cataclysms at long intervals apart. Three of these are frequently referred to (see Baldwin's Ancient America, p. 176). It is a curious confirmation that the Celts of Britain had a legend that part of their country once extended far into the Atlantic and was destroyed. Three catastrophes are mentioned in the Welsh traditions.

Quetzalcoatl, the Mexican Deity, is said to have come from "the distant east." He is described as a white man with a flowing beard. (N.B.— The Indians of North and South America are beardless.) He originated letters and regulated the Mexican calendar. After having taught them many peaceful arts and lessons he sailed away to the east in a canoe of serpent skins (see Short's North Americans of Antiquity, pp. 268-271), The same story is told of Zamna, the author of civilization in Yucatán.

The marvelous uniformity of the flood legends on all parts of the globe, alone remains to be dealt with. Whether these are some archaic versions of the story of the lost Atlantis and its submergence, or whether they are echoes of a great cosmic parable once taught and held in reverence in some common center whence they have reverberated throughout the world, does not immediately concern us. Sufficient for our purpose is to show the universal acceptance of these legends. It would be a needless waste of time and space to go over these flood stories one by one. Suffice it to say, that in India, Chaldea, Babylon, Media, Greece, Scandinavia, China, amongst the Jews and amongst the Keltic tribes of Britain, the legend is absolutely identical in all essentials. Now turn to the west and what do we find? The same story in its every detail pre-served amongst the Mexicans (each tribe having its own version), the people of Guatemala, Honduras, Perú, and almost every tribe of North American Indians. It is puerile to suggest that mere coincidence can account for this fundamental identity.

The following quotation from Le Plongeon's translation of the famous Troano MS., which may be seen in the British Museum, will appropriately bring this part of the subject to a case. The Troano MS. appears to have been written about 3,500 years ago, among the Mayas of Yucatán, and the following is its description of the catastrophe that submerged the island of Poseidonis: — "In the year 6 Kan, on the 11th Muluc in the month Zac, there occurred terrible earthquakes, which continued without interruption until the 13th Chuen. The country of the hills of mud, the land of Mu was sacrificed: being twice upheaved it suddenly disappeared during the night, the basin being continually shaken by volcanic forces. Being confined, caused the land to sink and rise several times in various places. At last, the surface gave way, and ten countries were torn asunder and scattered. Unable to stand the forces of the convulsions, they sank with their 64,000,000 of inhabitants 8060 years before the writing of this book."

But enough space has now been devoted to the fragments of evidence— all more or less convincing— which the world so far has been in possession of. Those interested in pursuing any special line of investigation are referred to the various works above named or quoted.

The subject in hand must now be dealt with. Drawn as they have been from contemporary records which were compiled and handed down through the ages we have to deal with, the facts here collected are based upon no assumption or conjecture. The writer may have failed fully to comprehend the facts, and so may have partially misstated them. But the original records are open for the investigation to the duly qualified, and those who are disposed to undertake the necessary training may obtain the powers to check and verify.

But even were all the occult records open to our inspection, it should be realized how fragmentary must be the sketch that attempts to summarize in a few pages the history of races and of nations extending over at least many hundreds of thousands of years. However, any details on such a subject— disconnected though they are— must be new and should therefore be interesting to the world at large.

Among the records above referred to there are maps of the world at various periods of its history, and it has been the great privilege of the writer to be allowed to obtain copies— more or less complete— of four of these. All four represent Atlantis and the surrounding lands at different epochs of their history. These epochs correspond approximately with the periods that lay between the catastrophes referred to above, and into the periods thus represented by the four maps the records of the Atlantean Race will naturally group themselves.

Before beginning the history of the race, however, a few remarks may be made about the geography of the four different epochs.

The first map represents the land surface of the earth as it existed about a million years ago, when the Atlantean Race was at its height, and before the first great submergence took place about 800,000 years ago. The continent of Atlantis itself, it will be observed, extended from a point a few degrees east of Iceland to about the site now occupied by Rio de Janeiro, in South America. Embracing Texas and the Gulf of México, the Southern and Eastern States of America, up to and including Labrador, it stretched across the ocean to our own islands — Scotland and Ireland, and a small portion of the north of England forming one of its promontories— while its equatorial lands embraced Brazil and the whole stretch of ocean to the African Gold Coast. Scattered fragments of what eventually became the continents of Europe, Africa, and

América, as well as remains of the still older, and once widespread continent of Lemuria, are also shown on this map. The remains of the still older Hyperborean continent, which was inhabited by the Second Root Race, are also given, and like Lemuria, colored blue.

As will be seen from the second map the catastrophe of 800,000 years ago caused very great changes in the land distribution of the globe. The great continent is now shorn of its northern regions, and its remaining portion has been still further rent. The now growing American continent is separated by a chasm from its parent continent of Atlantis, and this no longer comprises any of the lands now existing but occupies the bulk of the Atlantic basin from about 50o north to a few degrees south of the equator. The subsidence's and upheavals in other parts of the world have also been considerable— the British Islands for example, now being part of a huge island, which also embraces the Scandinavian peninsula, the north of France, and all the intervening and some of the surrounding seas. The dimensions of the remains of Lemuria it will be observed, have been further curtailed, while Europe, Africa and America have received accretions of territory. The third map shows the results of the catastrophe which took place about

The Story of Atlantis

200,000 years ago. With the exception of the rents in the contents both of Atlantis and América, and the submergence of Egypt, it will be seen how relatively unimportant the subsidence and upheavals at this epoch were, indeed the fact that this catastrophe has not always been considered as one of the great ones, is apparent from the quotation already given from the sacred book of the Guatemalans— three great ones only being there mentioned. The Scandinavian Island, however, appears now as joined to the mainland. The two islands into which Atlantis was now split were known by the names of Ruta and Daitya.

The stupendous character of the natural convulsion that took place about 80,000 years ago, will be apparent from the fourth map. Daitya, the smaller and more southerly of the islands, has almost entirely disappeared, while of Ruta there only remains the relatively small island of Poseidonis. This map was compiled about 75,000 years ago, and it no doubt fairly represents the land surface of the earth from that period onwards till the final submergence of Poseidonis in 9564 b. c., though during that period minor changes must have taken place. It will be noted that the land outlines had then begun to assume roughly the same appearance they do today, though the British Islands were still joined to the European continent, while the Baltic Sea was non-existent, and the Sahara Desert then formed part of the ocean floor.

Some reference to the very mystical subject of the Manus[13] is a necessary preliminary to the consideration of the origin of a Root Race. In Transaction No. 26, of the London Lodge, reference was invaded to the work done by these very exalted Beings, which embraces not only the planning of the types of the whole Manvantara but the superintending the formation and education of each Root Race in turn. The following quotation refers to these arrangements: "There are also Manus

---

[13] Manu is a term found as various meanings in Hinduism. In early texts, it refers to the archetypal man, or to the first man (progenitor of humanity). The Sanskrit term for 'human', मानव (IAST: mānava) means 'of Manu' or 'children of Manu'. In later texts, Manu is the title or name of fourteen rulers of the earth, or alternatively as the head of dynasties that begin with each cyclic Kalpa (aeon) when the universe is born anew. The title of the text Manusmriti uses this term as a prefix, but refers to the first Manu – Svayambhuva, the spiritual son of Brahma. In the earliest mention of Manu, in the Rigveda, Manu is only the ancestor of the "Five Peoples", or "Páñca Jánāḥ" (the five tribes being the Anu, Druhyus, Yadus, Turvashas, and Purus). The Aryans considered all other peoples to be a-manuṣa. Later, in Hindu cosmology, each Kalpa consists of fourteen Manvantaras, and each Manvantara is headed by a different Manu. The current universe is asserted to be ruled by the 7th Manu named Vaivasvata. Vaivasvata was the king of Dravida before the great flood. He was warned of the flood by the Matsya (fish) avatar of Vishnu, and built a boat that carried the Vedas, Manu's family, and the seven sages to safety, helped by Matsya. The tale is repeated with variations in other texts, including the Mahabharata and a few other Puranas. It is similar to other floods such as those associated with Gilgamesh and Noah.

whose duty it is to act in a similar way for each Root Race on each Planet of the Round, the Seed Manu planning the improvement in type which each successive Root Race inaugurates and the Root Manu actually incarnating amongst the new Race as a leader and teacher to direct the development and ensure the improvement."

The way in which the necessary segregation of the picked specimens is affected by the Manu in charge, and his subsequent care of the growing community, may be dealt with in a future Transaction. The merest reference to the mode of procedure is all that is necessary here.

It was of course from one of the sub-races of the Third Root Race on the continent, which is spoken of as Lemuria, that the segregation was affected which was destined to produce the Fourth Root Race. Following where necessary the history of the Race through the four periods represented by the four maps, it is proposed to divide the subject under the following headings:

1. Origin and territorial location of the different sub-races.

2. The political institutions they respectively evolved.

3. Their emigrations to other parts of the world.

4. The arts and sciences they developed.

5. The manners and customs they adopted.

6. The rise and decline amongst them of religious ideas.

The names of the different sub-races must first be given:

1. Rmoahal.

2. Tlavatli.

3. Toltec.

4. First Turanian.

5. Original Semite.

6. Akkadian.

7. Mongolian.

Some explanation is necessary as to the principle on which these names are chosen. Wherever modern ethnologists have discovered traces of one of these sub-races, or even identified a small part of one, the name they have given to it is used for the sake of simplicity, but in the case of the first two sub-races

The Story of Atlantis

there are hardly any traces left for science to seize upon, so the names by which they called themselves have been adopted.

Now the period represented by Map No. 1 shows the land surface of the earth as it existed about one million years ago, but the Rmoahal race carne into existence between four and five million years ago, at which period large portions of the great southern continent of Lemuria still existed, while the continent of Atlantis had not assumed the proportions it ultimately attained. It was upon a spur of this Lemurian land that the Rmoahal race was born. Roughly it may be located at latitude 70 north and longitude 50 west, which a reference to any modem atlas will show to lie on the Ashanti coast of today. It was a hot, moist country, where huge antediluvian animals lived in reedy swamps and dank forests. The fossil remains of such plants are today found in coal measures. The Rmoahals were a dark race— their complexion being a sort of mahogany black. Their height in these early days was about ten or twelve feet— truly a race of giants— but through the centuries their stature gradually dwindled, as did that of all the races in turn, and later on, we shall find they had shrunk to the stature of the "Furfooz man." They ultimately migrated to the southern shores of Atlantis, where they were engaged in constant warfare with the sixth and seventh sub-races of the Lemurians then inhabiting that country. A large part of the tribe eventually moved north, while the remainder settled down and intermarried with these black Lemurian aborigines. The result was that at the period we are dealing with— the first map period— there was no pure blood left in the south, and as we shall see it was from these dark races who inhabited the equatorial provinces, and the extreme south of the continent, that the Toltec conquerors subsequently drew their supplies of slaves. The remainder of the race, however, reached the extreme north-eastern promontories contiguous with Iceland and dwelling there for untold generations, they gradually became lighter in color, until at the date of the first map period we find them tolerably fair people. Their descendants eventually became subject, at least nominally, to the Semite kings.

That they dwelt there for untold generations is not meant to imply that their occupation was unbroken, for the stress of circum- stances at intervals of time drove them south. The cold of the glacial epochs of course operated alike with the other races, but the few words to be said on this subject may as well come in here.

The Story of Atlantis

Without going into the question of the different rotations which this earth performs, or the varying degrees of eccentricity of its orbit, a combination of which is sometimes held to be the cause of the glacial epochs, it is a fact— and one already recognized by some astronomers— that a minor glacial epoch occurs about every 30,000 years. But in addition to these there were two occasions in the history of Atlantis when the ice-belt desolated not merely the northern regions, but, invading the bulk of the continent, forced all life to migrate to equatorial lands. The first of these was in process during the Rmoahal days, about 3,000,000 years ago, while the second took place in the Toltec ascendency about 850,000 years ago.

With reference to all glacial epochs, it should be stated that though the inhabitants of northern lands were forced to settle during the winter far south of the ice-belt, there yet were great districts to which in summer they could return, and where for the sake of the hunting they encamped until driven south again by the winter cold.

The place of origin of the Tlavatli or 2nd sub-race was an island off the west coast of Atlantis. The spot is marked on the 1st map with the figure 2. Thence they spread into Atlantis proper, chiefly across the middle of the continent, gradually however tending northwards towards the stretch of coast facing the promontory of Greenland. Physically they were a powerful and haray race of a red-brown color, but they were not quite so tall as the Rmoahals whom they drove still further north. They were always mountain-loving people, .and their chief settlements were in the mountainous districts of the interior, which a comparison of Maps, 1 and 4 will show to be approximately conterminous with what ultimately became the island of Poseidonis. At this first map period they also— as just stated— peopled the northern coasts, whilst a mixture of Tlavatli and Toltec race inhabited the western islands, which subsequently formed part of the American continent.

We now come to the Toltec or 3rd sub-race. This was a magnificent development. It ruled the whole continent of Atlantis for thousands of years in great material power and glory. Indeed, so dominant and so endowed with vitality was this race that intermarriages with the following sub-races failed to modify the type, which still remained essentially Toltec; and hundreds of thousands of years later we find one of their remote family races ruling magnificently in México and Perú, long ages before their degenerate descendants were

The Story of Atlantis

conquered by the fiercer Aztec tribes from the north. The complexion of this race was also a red brown, but they were redder or more copper-colored than the Tlavatli. They also were a tall race, averaging about eight feet during the period of their ascendency, but of course dwindling, as all races did, to the dimensions that are common today. The type was an improvement on the two previous 'sub-races, the features being straight and well-marked, not unlike the ancient Greek. The approximate birthplace of this race may be seen, marked with the figure 3, on the first map. It lay near the west coast of Atlantis about latitude 30° North, and the whole of the surrounding country, embracing the bulk of the west coast of the continent, was peopled with a pure Toltec race. But as we shall see when dealing with the political organization, their territory eventually extended right across the continent, and it was from their great capital on the eastern coast that the Toltec emperors held their almost world-wide sway.

These first three sub-races are spoken of as the "red races," between whom and the four following there was not at first much mixture of blood. These four, though differing considerably from each other, have been called "yellow," and this color may appropriately define the complexion of the

Turanian and Mongolian, but the Semite and Akkadian were comparatively white.

The Turanian or 4th sub-race had their origin on the eastern side of the continent, south of the mountainous district inhabited by the Tlavatli people. This spot is marked 4 on Map No. 1. The Turanians were colonists from the earliest days, and great numbers migrated to the lands lying to the east of Atlantis. They were never a thoroughly dominant race on the mother- continent, though some of their tribes and family races became fairly powerful. The great central regions of the continent lying west and south of the Tlavatli mountainous district was their special though not their exclusive home, for they shared these lands with the Toltecs. The curious political and social experiments made by this sub-race will be dealt with later on.

As regards the original Semite or 5th sub-race ethnologists have been somewhat confused, as indeed it is extremely natural, they should be considering the very insufficient data they have to go upon. This sub-race had its origin in the mountainous country which formed the more southerly of the two north- eastern peninsulas which, as we have seen, is now represented by

Scotland, Ireland, and some of the surrounding seas. The site is marked 5 in Map No. 1. In this least desirable portion of the great continent the race grew and flourished, for centuries maintaining its independence against aggressive southern kings, till the time carne for it in turn to spread abroad and colonize. It must be remembered that by the time the Semites rose to power hundreds of thousands of years had passed and the 2nd map period had been reached. They were a turbulent, discontented race, always at war with their neighbors, especially with the then growing power of the Akkadians.

The birthplace of the Akkadian or 6th sub-race will be found on Map No. 2 (marked there with the figure 6), for it was after the great catastrophe of 800,000 years ago that this race first carne into existence. It took its rise in the land east of Atlantis, about the middle of the great peninsula whose south- eastern extremity stretched out towards the old continent. The spot may be located approximately at latitude 42o North and longitude 10o East. They did not for long, however, con- fine themselves to the land of their birth, but overran the now diminished continent of Atlantis. They fought with the Semites in many battles both on land and sea, and very considerable fleets were used on both sides. Finally about 100,000 years ago they completely vanquished the Semites, and from that time onwards an Akkadian dynasty was set up in the old Semite capital, and ruled the country wisely for several hundred years. They were a great trading sea-going, and colonizing people, and they established many centers of communication with distant lands.

The Mongolian or 7th sub-race seems to be the only one that had absolutely no touch with the mother-continent. Having its origin on the plains of Tartary (marked No. 7 on the second map) at about latitude 63o North and longitude 140o East, it was directly developed from descendants of the Turanian race, which it gradually supplanted over the greater part of Asia. This sub-race multiplied exceedingly, and even at the present day a majority of the earth's inhabitants technically belong to it, though many of its divisions are so deeply colored with the blood of earlier races as to be scarcely distinguishable from them.

Political Institutions. —In such a summary as this it would be impossible to describe how each sub-race was further sub-divided into nations, each having its distinct type and characteristics. All that can be here attempted is to sketch in broad outline the varying political institutions throughout the great

The Story of Atlantis

epochs of the race.

While recognizing that each sub-race as well as each Root Race is destined to stand in some respects at a higher level than the one before it, the cyclic nature of the development must be recognized as leading the race like the man through the various phases of infancy, youth, and manhood back to the infancy of old age again. Evolution necessarily means ultimate progress, even though the turning back of its ascending spiral may seem to make the history of politics or of religion a record not merely of development and progress but also of degradation and decay.

In making the statement therefore that its sub-race started under the most perfect government conceivable, it must be understood that this was owing to the necessities of their childhood, not to the merits of their matured manhood. For the Rmoahals were incapable of developing any plan of settled government, nor did they ever reach even as high a point of civilization as the 6th and 7th Lemurian sub-races. But the Manu who effected the segregation actually incarnated in the race and ruled it as king. Even when he no longer took visible part in the government of the race, Adept or Divine rulers were, when the times required it» still provided for the infant community. As students of Theosophy know, our humanity had not then reached the stage of development necessary to produce fully initiated Adepts. The rulers above referred to, including the Manu himself, were therefore necessarily the product of evolution on other systems of worlds.

The Tlavatli people showed some signs of advance in the art of government. Their various tribes or nations were ruled by chiefs or kings who generally received their authority by acclamation of the people. Naturally the most powerful individuals and greatest warriors were so chosen. A considerable empire was eventually established among them, in which one king became the nominal head, but bis suzerainty consisted rather in titular honor than in actual authority.

It was the Toltec race who developed the highest civilization and organized the most powerful empire of any of the Atlantean peoples, and it was then that the principle of hereditary succession was for the first time established. The race was at first divided into a number of petty independent kingdoms, constantly at war with each other, and all at war with the Lemurio-Rmoahals of the south. These were gradually conquered and made subject

The Story of Atlantis

peoples— many of their tribes being reduced to slavery. About one million years ago, however, these separate kingdoms united in a great federation with a recognized emperor at its head. This was of course inaugurated by great wars, but the outcome was peace and prosperity forth race.

It must be remembered that humanity was still for the most part possessed of psychic attributes, and by this time the most advanced had undergone the necessary training in the occult schools and had attained various stages of initiation— some even reaching to Adeptship. Now the second of these emperors was an Adept, and for thousands of years the Divine dynasty ruled not only all the kingdoms into which Atlantis was divided28but the islands on the west and the southern portion of the adjacent land lying to the east. When necessary, this dynasty was recruited from the Lodge of Initiates, but as a rule the power was handed down from father to son, all being more or less qualified, and the son in some cases receiving a further degree at the hands of his father. During all this period these Initiate rulers retained connection with the Occult Hierarchy which governs the world, submitting to its laws, and acting in harmony with its plans. This was the golden age of the Toltec race. The government was just and beneficent; the arts and sciences were cultivated— indeed the workers in these fields, guided as they were by occult knowledge, achieved tremendous results; religious belief and ritual was still comparatively pure — in fact the civilization of Atlantis had by this time reached its height.

After about 100,000 years of this golden age the degeneracy and decay of the race set in. Many of the tributary kings, and large numbers of the priests and people ceased to use their faculties and powers in accordance with the laws made by their Divine rulers, whose precepts and advice were now disregarded. Their connection with the Occult Hierarchy was broken. Personal aggrandizement, the attainment of wealth and authority, the humiliation and ruin of their enemies became more and more the objects towards which their occult powers were directed: and thus, turned from their lawful use, and practiced for all sorts of selfish and malevolent purposes, they inevitably led to what we must call by the name of sorcery.

Surrounded as this word is with the odium which credulity on the one hand and imposture on the other have during many centuries of superstition and ignorance gradually caused it to be associated, let us consider for a moment its real meaning, and the terrible effects which its practice is ever destined to bring on the world.

Partly through their psychic faculties, which were not yet quenched in the depths of materiality to which the race after- wards descended, and partly through their scientific attainments during this culmination of Atlantean civilization, the most intellectual and energetic members of the race gradually obtained more and more insight into the working of Nature's laws, and more and more control over some of her hidden forces. Now the desecration of this knowledge and its use for selfish ends is what constitutes sorcery. The awful effects, too, of such desecration are well enough exemplified in the terrible catastrophes that overtook the race. For when once the black practice was inaugurated it was destined to spread in ever widening circles. The higher spiritual guidance being thus withdrawn, the Karmic principie, which being the fourth, naturally reached its zenith during the Fourth Root Race, asserted itself more and more in humanity. Lust, brutality, and ferocity were all on the increase, and the animal nature in man was approaching its most degraded expression. lt was a moral question which from the very earliest times divided the Atlantean Race into two hostile camps, and what was begun in the Rmoahal times was terribly accentuated in the Toltec era. The battle of Armageddon is fought over and over again in every age of the world's history.

No longer submitting to the wise rule of the Initiate emperors, the followers of the "black arts " rose in rebellion and set up a rival emperor, who after much struggle and fighting drove the white emperor from his capital, the " City of the Golden Gates," and established himself on his throne.

The white emperor driven northward re-established himself in a city originally founded by the Tlavatli on the southern edge of the mountainous district, but which was now the seat of one of the tributary Toltec kings. He gladly welcomed the white emperor and placed the city at his disposal. A few more of the tributary kings also remained loyal to him, but most transferred their allegiance to the new emperor reigning at the old capital. These, however, did not long remain faithful. Constant assertions of independence were made by the tributary kings, and continual battles were fought in different parts of the empire, the practice of sorcery being largely resorted to, to supplement the powers of destruction possessed by the armies.

The Story of Atlantis

These events took place about 50,000 years before the first great catastrophe.

From this time onwards things went from bad to worse. The sorcerers used their powers more and more recklessly, and greater and greater numbers of people acquired and practiced these terrible "black arts."

Then carne the awful retribution when millions upon millions perished. The great "City of the Golden Gates" had by this time become a perfect den of iniquity. The waves swept over it and destroyed its inhabitants, and a black" emperor and his dynasty fell to rise no more. The emperor of the north as well as the initiated priests throughout the whole continent had long been fully aware of the evil days at hand, and subsequent pages will tell of the many priest-led emigrations which pre* ceded this catastrophe, as well as those of later date.

The continent was now terribly rent. But the actual amount of territory submerged by no means represented the damage done, for tidal waves swept over great tracts of land and left them desolate swamps. Whole provinces were rendered barren and remained for generations in an uncultivated and desert condition.

The remaining population too had received a terrible warning. It was taken to heart, and sorcery was for a time less pre- valent among them. A long period elapsed before any new powerful rule was established. We shall eventually find a Semite dynasty of sorcerers enthroned in the "City of the Golden Gates," but no Toltec power rose to eminence during the second map period. There were considerable Toltec populations still, but little of the pure blood remained on the mother continent.

On the island of Ruta however, in the third map period, a Toltec dynasty again rose to power and ruled through its tributary kings a large portion of the island. This dynasty was addicted to the black craft, which it must be understood became more and more prevalent during all three periods, until it culminated in the inevitable catastrophe, which to a great extent purified the earth of the monstrous evil. It must also be borne in mind that down to the very end when Poseidonis disappeared, an Initiate emperor or king— or at least one acknowledging the "good law"— held sway in some part of the island continent, acting under the guidance of the Occult Hierarchy in controlling where possible the evil sorcerers, and in guiding and instructing the small minority who were still willing to lead pure and wholesome lives. In later days this "white" king was as a rule elected by the priests— the handful, that is, who still followed the "good law."

Little more remains to be said about the Toltecs. In Poseidonis the population of the whole island was more or less mixed. Two kingdoms and one small republic in the west divided the island between them. The northern portion was ruled by an Initiate king. In the south too the hereditary principle had given way to election by the people. Exclusive race-dynasties were at an end, but kings of Toltec blood occasionally rose to power both in the north and south, the northern kingdom being constantly encroached upon by its southern rival, and more and more of its territory annexed.

Having dealt at some length with the state of things under the Toltecs, the leading political characteristics of the four following sub-races need not long detain us, for none of them reached the heights of civilization that the Toltecs did— in fact the degeneration of the race had set in.

It seems to have been some sort of feudal system that the natural bent of the Turanian race tended to develop. Each chief was supreme on his own territory, and the king was only primus inter pares. The chiefs who formed his council occasionally murdered their king and set up one of their own number in his place. They were a turbulent and lawless race— brutal and cruel also. The fact that at some periods of their history regiments of women took part in their wars is significant of the last-named characteristics.

But the strange experiment they made in social life which, but for its political origin, would more naturally have been dealt with under "manners and customs" is the most interesting fact in their record. Being continually worsted in war with their Toltec neighbors, knowing themselves to be greatly outnumbered, and desiring above all things increase of population, laws were passed, by which every man was relieved from the direct burden of maintaining his family. The State took charge of and provided for the children, and they were looked upon as its property. This naturally tended to increase the birth-rate amongst the Turanians, and the ceremony of marriage carne to be disregarded. The ties of family life, and the feeling of parental love were of course destroyed, and the scheme having been found to be a failure, was ultimately given up. Other attempts at finding socialistic solutions of economic problems which still vex us to-day, were tried and abandoned by this race.

It was in the third map period, about 100,000 years ago, that the Akkadians finally overthrew the Semite power. This 6th sub-race was a much more law-abiding people than their predecessors. Traders and sailors, they lived in settled com- munities, and naturally produced an oligarchical form of government. A peculiarity of theirs, of which Sparta is the only modern example, was the dual system of two kings reigning in one city. As a result, probably of their sea-going taste, the study of the stars became a characteristic pursuit, and this race made great advances both in astronomy and astrology.

The Mongolian people were an improvement on their immediate ancestors of the brutal Turanian stock. Born as they were on the wide steppes of Eastern Siberia, they never had any touch with the mother-continent, and owing, doubtless, to their environment, they became a nomadic people. More psychic and more religious than the Turanians from whom they sprang, the form of government towards which they gravitated required a suzerain in the background who should be supreme both as aterritorial ruler and as a chief high priest.

Emigrations. —Three causes contributed to produce

emigrations. The Turanian race, as we have seen, was from its very start imbued with the spirit of colonizing, which it carried out on a considerable scale. The Semites and Akkadians were also to a certain extent colonizing races.

Then, as time went on and population tended more and more to outrun the limits of subsistence, necessity operated with the least well-to-do in every race alike and drove them to seek for a livelihood in less thickly populated countries. For it should be realized that when the Atlanteans reached their zenith in the Toltec era, the proportion of population to the square miles on the continent of Atlantis probably equaled, even if it did not exceed, our modern experience in England and Belgium. It is at all events certain that the vacant spaces available for colonization were very much larger in that age than in ours, while the total population of the world, which at the present moment is probably not more than twelve hundred to fifteen hundred million, amounted in those days to the big figure of about two thousand million.

Lastly, there were the priest-led emigrations which took place prior to each catastrophe— and there were many more of these than the four great ones referred to above. The initiated kings and priests who followed the "good law" were aware beforehand of the impending calamities. Each one, therefore, naturally became a center of prophetic warning, and ultimately a leader of a band of colonists. It may be noted here that in later days the rulers of the country deeply resented these priest-led emigrations, as tending to impoverish and depopulate their kingdoms, and it became necessary for the emigrants to get on board ship secretly during the night.

In roughly tracing the lines of emigration followed by each sub-race in turn, we shall of necessity ultimately reach the lands which their respective descendants today occupy.

For the earliest emigrations we must go back to the Rmoahal days. It will be remembered that that portion of the race which inhabited the northeastern coasts alone retained its purity of blood. Harried on their southern borders and driven further north by the Tlavatli warriors, they began to overflow to the neighboring land to the east, and to the still nearer promontory of Greenland. In the second map period no pure Rmoahals were left on the then reduced mother-continent, but the northern promontory of the continent then rising on the west was occupied by them, as well as the

Greenland cape35already mentioned, and the western shores of the great Scandinavian Island. There was also a colony on the land lying north of the central Asian sea.

Brittany and Picardy then formed part of the Scandinavian Island, while the island itself became in the third map period part of the growing continent of Europe. Now it is in France that remains of this race have been found in the quaternary strata, and the brachycephalies, or round-headed specimen known as the "Furfooz man," may be taken as a fair average of the type of the race in its decay.

Many times, forced to move south by the rigors of a glacial epoch, many times driven north by the greed of their more powerful neighbors, the scattered and degraded remnants of this race may be found to-day in the modern Lapps, though even here there was some infusion of other blood. And so it comes to pass that these faded and stunted specimens of humanity are the lineal descendants of the black race of giants who arose on the equatorial lands of Lemuria well-nigh five million years ago.

The Tlavatli colonists seem to have spread out towards every point of the compass. By the second map period their descendants were settled on the western shores of the then growing American continent (California) as well as on its extreme southern coasts (Rio de Janeiro). We also find them occupying the eastern shores of the Scandinavian Island, while numbers of them sailed across the ocean, rounded the coast of Africa, and reached India. There, mixing with the indigenous Lemurian population, they formed the Dravidian race. In later days this in its turn received an infusion of Aryan or Fifth Race blood, from which results the complexity of type found in India today. In fact, we have here a very fair example of the extreme difficulty of deciding any question of race upon merely physical evidence, for it would be quite possible to have Fifth Race egos incarnate among the Brahmans, Fourth Race egos among the lower castes, and some lingering Third Race among the hill tribes.

By the fourth map period we find a Tlavatli people occupying the southern parts of South América, from which it may be inferred that the Patagonians probably had remote Tlavatli ancestry.

Remains of this race, as of the Rmoahals, have been found in the quaternary strata of Central Europe, and the dolichocephalous "Cro-Magnon man"[14] may be taken as an average specimen of the race in its decadence, while the "Lake-Dwellers" of Switzerland formed an even earlier and not quite pure offshoot. The only people who can be cited as fairly pure- blooded specimens of the race at the present day are some of the brown tribes of Indians of South América. The Burmese and Siamese have also Tlavatli blood in their veins, but in their case, it was mixed with, and therefore dominated by, the nobler stock of one of the Aryan sub-races.

We now come to the Toltecs. It was chiefly to the west that their emigrations tended, and the neighboring coasts of the American continent were in the second map period peopled by a pure Toltec race, the greater part of those left on the mother-continent being then of very mixed blood. It was on the continents of North and South América that this race spread abroad and flourished, and on which thousands of years later were established the empires of México and Perú. The great- ness of these empires is a matter of history, or at least of

---

[14] Students of geology and paleontology will know that these sciences regard the "Cro-Magnon man" as prior to the "Furfooz" and seeing that the two races ran alongside each other for vast periods of time, it may quite well be that the individual " Cro-Magnon " skeleton, though representative of the second race, was deposited in the quaternary strata thousands of years before the individual Furfooz man lived on the earth.

tradition supplemented by such evidence as is afforded by magnificent architectural remains. It may here be noted that while the Mexican empire was for centuries great and powerful in all that is usually regarded as power and greatness in our civilization of to-day, it never reached the height attained by the Peruvians about 14,000 years ago under their Inca sovereigns, for as regards the general well-being of the people, the justice and beneficence of the government, the equitable nature of the land tenure, and the pure and religious life of the inhabitants, the Peruvian empire of those days might be considered a traditional though the faint echo of the golden age of the Toltecs on the mother-continent of Atlantis.

The average Red Indian of North or South América is the best representative to-day of the Toltec people, but of course bears no comparison with the highly civilized individual of the race at its zenith.

Egypt must now be referred to, and the consideration of this subject should let in a flood of light upon its early history. Although the first settlement in that country was not in the strict sense of the term a colony, it was from the Toltec race that was subsequently drawn the first great body of emigrants intended to mix with and dominate the aboriginal people.

In the first instance it was the transfer of a great Lodge of Initiates. This took place about 400,000 years ago. The golden age of the Toltecs was long past. The first great catastrophe had taken place. The moral degradation of the people and the consequent practice of the "black arts " were becoming more accentuated and widely spread. Purer surroundings for the White Lodge were needed. Egypt was isolated and was thinly peopled, and therefore Egypt was chosen. The settlement so made answered its purpose, and undisturbed by adverse conditions the Lodge of Initiates for nearly 200,000 years did its work.

About 210,000 years ago, when the time was ripe, the Occult Lodge founded an empire— the first "Divine Dynasty" of Egypt— and began to teach the people. Then it was that the first great body of colonists was brought from Atlantis, and sometime during the ten thousand years that led up to the second catastrophe, the two great Pyramids of Gizeh were built, partly to provide permanent Halls of Initiation, but also to act as treasure-house and shrine for some great talisman of power during the submergence which the Initiates knew to be impending. Map No. 3 shows Egypt at that date as

The Story of Atlantis

under water. It remained so for a considerable period, but on its re- emergence, it was again peopled by the descendants of many of its old inhabitants who had retired to the Abyssinian mountains (shown in Map No. 3 as an island) as well as by fresh bands of Atlantean colonists from various parts of the world. A considerable immigration of Akkadians then helped to modify the Egyptian type. This is the era of the second "Divine Dynasty" of Egypt— the rulers of the country being again initiated adepts.

The catastrophe of 80,000 years ago again laid the country under water, but this time it was only a temporary wave. When it receded the third "Divine Dynasty"— that mentioned by Manetho— began its rule, and it was under the early kings of this dynasty that the great Temple of Karnak and many of the more ancient buildings still standing in Egypt were constructed. In fact with the exception of the two pyramids no building in Egypt predates the catastrophe of 80,000 years ago.

The final submergence of Poseidonis sent another tidal wave over Egypt. This too, was only a temporary calamity, but it brought the Divine Dynasties to an end, for the Lodge of Initiates had transferred its quarters to other lands.

Various points here left untouched have already been dealt with in the Transaction of the London Lodge "The Pyramids and Stonehenge."

The Turanians who in the first map period had colonized the northern parts of the land lying immediately to the east of Atlantis, occupied in the second map period its southern shores (which included present Morocco and Algeria). We also find them wandering eastwards, and both the east and west coasts of the central Asian sea were peopled by them. Bands of them ultimately moved still further east, and the nearest approximation to the type of this race is to-day to be found in the inland Chinese. A curious freak of destiny must be recorded about one of their western offshoots. Dominated all through the centuries by their more powerful Toltec neighbors, it was yet reserved for a small branch of the Turanian stock to conquer and replace the last great empire that the Toltecs raised, for the brutal and barely civilized Aztecs were of pure Turanian blood.

The Semite emigrations were of two kinds, first, those which were controlled by the natural impulse of the race: second, that special emigration which was effected under the direct guidance of the Manu; for, strange as it may seem, it was not from

The Story of Atlantis

the Toltecs but from this lawless and turbulent toughly vigorous and energetic sub-race that was chosen the nucleus destined to be developed into our great Fifth or Aryan Race. The reason, no doubt, lay in the Manasic[15] characteristic with which the number five is always associated. The sub-race of that number was inevitably developing its physical brain power and intellect, although at the expense of the psychic perceptions, while that same development of intellect to infinitely higher levels is at once the glory and the destined goal of our Fifth Root Race.

Dealing first with the natural emigrations we find that in the second map period while still leaving powerful nations on the mother continent, the Semites had spread both west and east-west to the lands now forming the United States, thus accounting for the Semitic-type to be found in some of the Indian races, and east to the northern shores of the neighboring continent, which combined all there then was of Europe, Africa, and Asia. The type of the ancient Egyptians, as well as of other neighboring nations, was to some extent modified by this original Semitic blood; but with the exception of the Jews, the only representatives

---

[15] The mind: that which distinguishes man from the animals.

of the comparatively unmixed race at the present day are the lighter colored Kabyle[16] of the Algerian mountains.

The tribes resulting from the segregation effected by the Manu for the formation of the new Root Race eventually found their way to the southern shores of the central Asian sea, and there the first great Aryan kingdom was established. When the Transaction dealing with the origin of a Root Race comes to be written, it will be seen that many of the peoples we are accustomed to call Semitic are really Aryan in blood. The world will also be enlightened as to what constitutes the claim of the Hebrews to be considered a "chosen people." Shortly it may be stated that they constitute an abnormal and unnatural Jink between the Fourth and Fifth Root Races.

---

[16] Kabyle People are a Berber ethnic group indigenous to Kabylia in the north of Algeria, spread across the Atlas Mountains, 160 kilometers (100 mi) east of Algiers. They represent the largest Berber-speaking population of Algeria and the second largest in North Africa.

Many of the Kabyles have emigrated from Algeria, influenced by factors such as the Algerian Civil War,[5] cultural repression by the central Algerian government,[6] and overall industrial decline. Their diaspora has resulted in Kabyle people living in numerous countries. Large populations of Kabyle people settled in France and, to a lesser extent, Canada (mainly Québec) and United States. The Kabyle people speak Kabyle, a Berber language. Since the Berber Spring of 1980, they have been at the forefront of the fight for the official recognition of Berber languages in Algeria.

The Story of Atlantis

The Akkadians, though eventually becoming supreme rulers on the mother continent of Atlantis, owed their birthplace as we have seen in the second map period, to the neighboring continent— that part occupied by the basin of the Mediterranean about the present island of Sardinia being their special home. From this center they spread eastwards, occupying what eventually became the shores of the Levant, and reaching as far as Persia and Arabia. As we have seen, they also helped people in Egypt. The early Etruscans, the Phoenicians, including the Carthaginians and the Sumero-Akkads, were branches of this race, while the Basques of to-day have probably more of the Akkadian than of any other blood which flows in their veins.

A reference to the early inhabitants of our own islands may4iappropriately be made here, for it was in the early Akkadian days, about 100,000 years ago, that the colony of Initiates who founded Stonehenge landed on these shores— "these shores " being, of course, the shores of the Scandinavian part of the continent of Europe, as shown in Map No. 3. The initiated priests and their followers appear to have belonged to a very early strain of the Akkadian race— they were taller, fairer, and longer headed than the aborigines of the country, who

75

were a very mixed race, but mostly degenerate remnants of the Rmoahals. As readers of the Transaction of the London Lodge on the "Pyramids and Stonehenge," will know, the rude simplicity of Stone-henge was intended as a protest against the extravagant ornament and over-decoration of the existing temples in Atlantis, where the debased worship of their own images was being carried on by the inhabitants.

The Mongolians, as we have seen, never laid any touch with the mother-continent. Born on the wide plains of Tartary, their emigrations for long found ample scope within those regions; but more than once tribes of Mongol descent have overflowed from northern Asia to America, across Behring's Straits, and the last of such emigrations— that of the Kitans, some 1,300 years ago— has left traces which some western savants have been able to follow. The presence of Mongolian blood in some tribes of North American Indians has also been recognized by various writers on ethnology. The Hungarians and Malays are both known to be offshoots of this race, ennobled in the one case by a strain of Aryan blood, degraded in the other by mixture with the effete Lemurians. But the interesting fact about the Mongolians is that its last family race is still in full force— it has not in fact yet reached its zenith— and the Japanese nation has still got history to give to the world.

Arts and Sciences. —It must primarily be recognized that our own Aryan race has naturally achieved far greater results in almost every direction than did the Atlanteans, but even where they failed to reach our level, the records of what they accomplished are of interest as representing the high water mark which their tide of civilization reached. On the other hand, the character of the scientific achievements in which they did outstrip us are of so dazzling a nature, that bewilderment at such unequal development is apt to be the feeling left.

The arts and sciences, as practiced by the first two races, were, of course, crude in the extreme, but we do not propose to follow the progress achieved by each sub-race separately. The history of the Atlantean, as of the Aryan race, was interspersed with periods of progress and of decay. Eras of culture were followed by times of lawlessness, during which all artistic and scientific development was lost, these again being succeeded by civilizations reaching to still higher levels. It must naturally be with the periods of culture that the following remarks will deal, chief among which stands out the great Toltec era.

Architecture and sculpture, painting and music were all practiced in Atlantis. The music even at the best of times was crude, and the instruments of the most primitive type. All the Atlantean races were fond of color, and brilliant hues decorated both the insides and the outsides of their houses but painting as a fine art was never well established, though in the later days some kind of drawing and painting was taught in the schools. Sculpture on the other hand, which was also taught in the schools, was widely practiced, and reached great excellence. As we shall see later on under the head of "Religion" it became customary for every man who could afford it to place in one of the temples an image of himself. These were sometimes carved in wood or in hard black stone like basalt, but among the wealthy, it became the fashion to have their statues cast in one of the precious metals, orichalcum, gold, or silver. A very fair resemblance of the individual usually resulted, while in some cases a striking likeness was achieved.

Architecture, however, was naturally the most widely practiced of these arts. Their buildings were massive structures of gigantic proportions. The dwelling houses in the cities were not, as ours are,

The Story of Atlantis

closely crowded together in streets. Like their country houses some stood in their own garden grounds, others were separated by plots of common land, but all were isolated structures. In the case of houses of any importance four blocks of building surrounded a central courtyard, in the center of which generally stood one of the fountains whose number in the "City of the Golden Gates" gained for it the second appellation of the "City of Waters." There was no exhibition of goods for sale as in modern streets. All transactions of buying and selling took place privately, except at stated times, when large public fairs were held in the open spaces of the cities. But the characteristic feature of the Toltec house was the tower that rose from one of its corners or from the center of one of the blocks. A spiral staircase built outside led to the upper stories, and a pointed dome terminated the tower—this upper portion being very commonly used as an observatory. As already stated, the houses were decorated with bright colors. Some were ornamented with carvings, others with frescoes or painted patterns. The window-spaces were filled with some manufactured article similar to, but less transparent than, glass. The interiors were not furnished with the elaborate detail of our modern dwellings, but the life was highly civilized of its kind.

The temples were huge halls resembling more than anything else the gigantic piles of Egypt but built on a still more stupendous scale. The pillars supporting the roof were generally square, seldom circular. In the days of the decadence the aisles were surrounded with innumerable chapels in which were enshrined the statues of the more important inhabitants. These side shrines indeed were occasionally of such considerable size as to admit a whole retinue of priests whom some especially great man might have in his service for the ceremonial worship of his image. Like the private houses the temples too were never complete without the dome-capped towers, which of course were of corresponding size and magnificence. These were used for astronomical observations and for sun-worship.

The precious metals were largely used in the adornment of the temples, the interiors being often not merely inlaid but plated with gold. Gold and silver were highly valued, but as we shall see later on when the subject of the currency is dealt with, the uses to which they were put were entirely artistic and had nothing to do with coinage, while the great quantities that were then produced by the chemists— or as we should nowadays call them alchemists— may be said to have taken them out of the category of the precious metals. This power of transmutation of metals was not universal, but it was so widely possessed that enormous quantities were made. In fact, the production of the wished-for metals may be regarded as one of the industrial enterprises of those days by which these alchemists gained their living. Gold was admired even more than silver and was consequently produced in much greater quantity.

Education. —A few words on the subject of language will fitly preclude consideration of the training in the schools and colleges of Atlantis. During the first map period, Toltec was the universal language, not only throughout the continent but in the western islands and that part of the eastern continent which recognized the emperor's rule. Remains of the Rmoahal and Tlavatli speech survived it is true in out-of-the-way parts, just as the Keltic and Cymric speech survives to-day among us in Ireland and Wales. The Tlavatli tongue was the basis used by the Turanians, who introduced such modifications that an entirely different language was in time produced; while the45Semites and Akkadians, adopting a Toltec groundwork, modified it in their respective ways, and so produced two divergent varieties. Thus, in the later days of Poseidonis, there were several entirely different languages— all however belonging to the agglutinative type— for it was not till the Fifth Race days that the descendants of the Semites and Akkadians developed inflectional speech. All through the ages, however, the Toltec language fairly maintained its purity, and the same tongue that was spoken in Atlantis in the days of its splendor was used, with but slight alterations, thousands of years later in México and Perú.

The schools and colleges of Atlantis in the great Toltec days, as well as in subsequent eras of culture, were all endowed by the State. Though every child was required to pass through the primary school, the subsequent training differed very widely. The primary schools formed a sort of winnowing ground. Those who showed real aptitude for study were, along with the children of the dominant classes who naturally had greater abilities, drafted into the higher schools at about the age of twelve. Reading and writing, which were regarded as mere preliminaries, had already been taught them in the primary schools.

But reading and writing were not considered necessary for the great masses of the inhabitants who had to spend their lives in tilling the land, or in handicrafts, the practice of which was required by the community. The great majority of the children therefore were at once passed on to the technical schools best suited to their various abilities. Chief among these were the agricultural schools. Some branches of mechanics also formed part of the training, while in outlying districts and by the sea-side hunting and fishing were naturally included. And so, the children all received the education or training which was most appropriate for them.

The children of superior abilities, who as we have seen had been taught to read and write, had a much more elaborate education. The properties of plants and their healing qualities formed an important branch of study. There were no recognized physicians in those days— every educated man knew more or less of medicine as well as of magnetic healing. Chemistry, mathematics, and astronomy were also taught. The training in such studies finds its analogy among us, but the object towards which the teachers' efforts were mainly directed, was the development of the pupil's psychic faculties and his instruction in the more hidden forces of nature. The occult properties of plants, metals, and precious stones, as well as the alchemical processes of transmutation, were included in this category. But as time went on it became more and more the personal power, which Bulwer Lytton calls vril, and the operation of which he has fairly accurately described in his Coming Race^ that the colleges for the higher training of the youth of Atlantis were specially occupied in developing. The marked change which took place when the decadence of the race set in was, that instead of merit and aptitude being regarded as warrants for advancement to the higher grades of instruction, the dominant classes becoming more and more exclusive allowed none but their own children to graduate in the higher knowledge which gave so much power.

In such an empire as the Toltec, agriculture naturally received much attention. Not only were the laborers taught their duties in technical schools, but colleges were established in which the knowledge necessary for carrying out experiments in the crossing both of animals and plants, were taught to fitting students.

As readers of Theosophic literature may know, wheat was not evolved on this planet at all. It was the gift of the Manu who brought it from another globe outside our chain of worlds. But oats and some of our other cereals are the results of crosses between wheat and the indigenous grasses of the earth. Now the experiments which gave these results were carried out in the agricultural schools of Atlantis. Of, course such experiments were guided by high knowledge. But the most notable achievement to be recorded of the Atlantean agriculturists was the evolution of the plantain or banana. In the original wild state, it was like an elongated melon with scarcely any pulp, but full of seeds as a melon is. It was of course only by centuries (if not thousands of years) of continuous selection and elimination that the present seedless plant evolved.

Among the domesticated animals of the Toltec days were creatures that looked like very small tapirs. They naturally fed upon roots or herbage, but like the pigs of today, which they resembled in more than one particular, they were not over cleanly and ate whatever came in their way. Large cat-like animals and the wolf-like ancestors of the dog might also be met about human habitations. The Toltec carts appear to have been drawn by creatures somewhat resembling small camels. The Peruvian llamas of today are probably their descendants. The ancestors of the Irish elk, too, roamed in herds about the hillsides in much the same way as our

High-land cattle do now— too wild to allow of easy approach, but still under the control of man.

Constant experiments were made in breeding and cross- breeding different kinds of animals, and, curious though it may seem to us, artificial heat was largely used to force their development, so that the results of crossing and interbreeding might be more quickly apparent. The use, too, of different colored lights in the chambers where such experiments were carried on were adopted in order to obtain varying results.

This control and molding at will by a man of the animal forms brings us to a rather startling and very mysterious subject. Reference has been made above to the work done by the Manus. Now it is in the mind of the Manu that originates all improvements in type and the potentialities latent in every form of being. In order to work out in detail the improvements in the animal forms, the help, and cooperation of man were required. The amphibian and reptile forms that then abounded had about run their course and were ready to assume the more advanced type of bird or mammal. These forms constituted the inchoate material placed at man's disposal, and the clay was ready to assume whatever shape the potter's hands might mold it into. It was

The Story of Atlantis

especially with animals in the intermediate stage that so many of the experiments above referred to were tried, and doubtless, the domesticated animals like the horse, which are now of such service to man, are the result of these experiments in which the men of those days acted in co-operation with the Manu and his ministers. But the co-operation was too soon withdrawn. Selfishness obtained the upper hand, and war and discord brought the Golden Age of the Toltecs to a cióse. When instead of working loyally for a common end, under the guidance of their Initiate kings, men began to prey upon each other, the beasts which might gradually have assumed, under the care of man, more and more useful and domesticated forms, being left to the guidance of their own instincts naturally followed the example of their monarch and began to prey upon each other. Some indeed had actually already been trained and used by men in their hunting expeditions, and thus the semi-domesticated cat-like animals above referred to naturally became the ancestors of the leopards and jaguars.

One illustration of what some may be tempted to call a fantastic theory, though it may not elucidate the problem, will at least point the moral contained in this supplement to our knowledge regarding the mysterious manner in which our evolution has proceeded. The lion it would appear might have had a gentler nature and a less fierce aspect had the men of those days completed the task that was given to them to perform. Whether or not he is fated eventually "to lie down with the lamb and eat straw like the ox" the destiny in store for him as pictured in the mind of the Manu has not yet been realized, for the picture was that of a powerful but domesticated animal — a strong level-backed creature, with large intelligent eyes, intended to act as man's most powerful servant for purposes of traction.

The "City of the Golden Gates" and its surroundings must be described before we come to consider the marvelous system by which its inhabitants were supplied with water. It lay, as we have seen, on the east coast of the continent close to the sea, and about 15o north of the equator. A beautifully wooded park-like country surrounded the city. Scattered over a large area of this were the villa residences of the wealthier classes. To the west lay a range of mountains, from which the water supply of the city was drawn. The city itself was built on the slopes of a hill, which rose from the plain about 500 feet. On the summit of this hill lay the emperor's palace and gardens, in the center of which welled up from the earth a never-ending stream of water, supplying first the palace and the fountains in the gardens, thence flowing in the four directions and falling in cascades into a canal or moat which encompassed the palace grounds, and thus separated them from the city which lay below on every side. From this canal, four channels led the water through four-quarters of the city to cascades which in their turn supplied another encircling canal at a lower level. There were three such canals forming con- centric circles, the outermost and lowest of which was still above the level of the plain. The fourth canal at this lowest level, but on a rectangular plan, received the constantly flowing waters, and in its turn discharged them into the sea. The city extended over part of the plain, up to the edge of this great outermost moat, which surrounded and defended it with a line of waterways extending about twelve miles by ten miles square.

It will thus be seen that the city was divided into three great belts, each hemmed in by its canals. The characteristic feature of the upper belt that lay just below the palace grounds, was a circular racecourse and large public gardens. Most of the houses of the court officials also lay on this belt, and here also was an institution of which we have no parallel in modern times. The term "Strangers Home" amongst us suggests mean appearance and sordid surroundings, but this was a palace where all strangers who might come to the city were entertained as long as they might choose to stay— being treated all the time as guests of the Government. The detached houses of the inhabitants and the various temples scattered throughout the city occupied the other two belts. In the days of the Toltec greatness there seems to have been no real poverty— even the retinue of slaves attached to most houses being well fed and clothed— but there were a number of comparatively poor houses in the lowest belt to the north, as well as outside the outermost canal towards the sea. The inhabitants of this part were mostly connected with the shipping, and their houses though detached were built closer together than in other districts.

It will be seen from the above that the inhabitants had thus a never-failing supply of pure clear water constantly coursing through the city, while the upper belts and the emperor's palace were protected by lines of moats, each one at a higher level as the center was approached.

Now it does not require much mechanical

knowledge in order to realize how stupendous must have been the works needed to provide this supply, for in the days of its greatness the "City of the Golden Gates" embraced within its four circles of moats over two million inhabitants. No such system of water supply has ever been attempted in Greek, Román or modern times— indeed it is very doubtful whether our ablest engineers, even at the expenditure of untold wealth, could produce such a result.

A description of some of its leading features will be of interest. It was from a lake that lay among the mountains to the west of the city, at an elevation of about 2,600 feet, that the supply was drawn. The main aqueduct, which was of oval section, measuring fifty feet by thirty feet, led underground to an enormous heart-shaped reservoir. This lay deep below the palace, in fact at the very base of the bill on which the palace and the city stood. From this reservoir, a perpendicular shaft of about 500 feet up through the solid rock gave passage to the water which welled up in the palace grounds, and thence was dis- tributed throughout the city. Various pipes from the central reservoir also led to different parts of the city to supply drinking water and public fountains. Systems of sluices of course also existed to control or cut off the supply of the different districts.

From the above, it will be apparent to anyone possessed of some little knowledge of mechanics that the pressure in the subterranean aqueduct and the central reservoir from which the water naturally rose to the basin in the palace gardens, must have been enormous, and the resisting power of the material used in their construction consequently prodigious.

If the system of water supply in the "City of the Golden Gates" was wonderful, the Atlantean methods of locomotion must be recognized as still more marvelous, for the airship or flying machine which Keely in América and Maxim in this country are now attempting to produce, was then a realized fact. It was not at any time a common means of transport the slaves, the servants, and the masses who labored with their hands had to trudge along the country tracks or travel in rude carts with solid wheels drawn by uncouth animals. The airboats may be considered as the private carriages of those days, or rather the private yachts, if we regard the relative number of those who possessed them, for they must have been at all times difficult and costly to produce. They were not as a rule built to accommodate many persons. Numbers were constructed for only two, some allowed for six or eight passengers. In the later days when war and strife had brought the Golden Age to an end, battleships that could navigate the air had to a great extent replaced the battleships at sea— having naturally proved far more powerful engines of destruction. These were constructed to carry as many as fifty, and in some cases even up to a hundred fighting men.

The material of which the airboats were constructed was either wood or metal. The earlier ones were built of wood— the boards used to be exceedingly thin, but the injection of some substance which did not add materially to the weight while it gave leather-like toughness, provided the necessary combination of lightness and strength. When metal was used it was generally an alloy— two white-colored metals and one red one entering into its composition. The resultant was white-colored, like aluminum, and even lighter in weight. Over the rough framework of the airboat was extended a large sheet of this metal which was then beaten into shape and electrically welded where necessary. But whether built of metal or wood their outside surface was apparently seamless and perfectly smooth, and they shone in the dark as if coated with luminous paint.

In shape they were boat-like, but they were invariably decked over, for when at full speed it could not have been convenient, even if safe, for any on board to remain on the upper deck. Their propelling and steering gear could be brought into use at either end.

But the all-interesting question is that relates to the power by which they were propelled. In the earlier times, it seems to have been personal vril that supplied the motive power— whether used in conjunction with any mechanical contrivance matters not much— but in the later days, this was replaced by a force which, though generated in what is to us an unknown manner, operated nevertheless through definite mechanical arrangements. This force, though not yet discovered by science, more nearly approached that which Keely in America is learning to handle than the electric power used by Maxim. It was in fact of an etheric nature, but though we are no nearer to the solution of the problem, its method of operation can be described. The mechanical arrangements no doubt differed somewhat in different vessels. The following description is taken from an airboat in which on one occasion three ambassadors from the king who ruled over the northern part of Poseidonis made the journey to the court of the

The Story of Atlantis

southern kingdom. A strong heavy metal chest which lay in the center of the boat was the generator. Thence the force flowed through two large flexible tubes to either end of the vessel, as well as through eight subsidiary tubes fixed fore and aft to the bulwarks. These had double openings pointing vertically both up and down. When the journey was about to begin the valves of the eight bulwark tubes which pointed downwards were opened— all the other valves being closed. The current rushing through these impinged on the earth with such force as to drive the boat up- wards, while the air itself continued to supply the necessary fulcrum. When a sufficient elevation was reached the flexible tube at that end of the vessel which pointed away from the desired destination, was brought into action, while by the partial closing of the valves the current rushing through the5reight vertical tubes was reduced to the small amount required to maintain the elevation reached. The great volume of the current, being now directed through the large tube pointing downwards from the stern at an angle of about forty-five degrees, while helping to maintain the elevation, also provided the great motive power to propel the vessel through the air. The steering was accomplished by the discharge of the current through this tube, for the slightest change in its direction at once caused an alteration in the vessel's course. But constant supervision was not required. When a long journey had to be taken the tube could be fixed so as to need no handling till the destination was almost reached. The maximum speed attained was about one hundred miles an hour, the course of flight never being a straight line, but always in the form of long waves, now approaching and now receding from the earth. The elevation at which the vessels travelled was only a few hundred feet— indeed, when high mountains lay in the line of their track it was necessary to change their course and go round them— the more rarefied air no longer supplying the necessary fulcrum. Hills of about one thousand feet were the highest they could cross. The means by which the vessel was brought to a stop on reaching its destination— and this could be done equally well in mid-air— was to give escape to some of the current force through the tube at that end of the boat which pointed towards its destination, and the current impinging on the land or air in front, acted as a drag, while the propelling force behind was gradually reduced by the closing of the valve. The reason has still to be given for the existence of the eight tubes pointing upwards from the bulwarks. This had more specially to do with the aerial warfare. Having so powerful a force at their disposal, the warships naturally directed the current against each other. Now, this was apt to destroy the equilibrium of the ship so struck and to turn it upside down— a situation sure to be taken advantage of by the enemy's vessel to make an attack with her ram. There was also the further danger of being precipitated to the ground unless the shutting and opening of the necessary valves were quickly attended to. In whatever position the vessel might be, the tubes pointing towards the earth were naturally those through which the current should be rushing, while the tubes pointing upwards should be closed. The means by which a vessel turned upside down might be righted and placed again on a level keel, was accomplished by using the four tubes pointing downwards at one side of the vessel only, while the four at the other side were kept closed. The Atlanteans had also seagoing vessels which were propelled by some power analogous to that above mentioned, but the current force which was eventually found to be most effective in this case had a denser appearance than that used in the airboats.

Manners and Customs.—There was doubtless as much variety in the manners and customs of the Atlanteans at different epochs of their history, as there has been among the various nations which compose our Aryan race. With the fluctuating fashion of the centuries, we are not concerned. The following remarks will attempt to deal merely with the leading characteristics which differentiate their habits from our own, and these will be chosen as much as possible from the great Toltec era.

With regard to marriage and the relations of the sexes, the experiments made by the Turanians have already been referred to. Polygamous customs were prevalent at different times among all the sub-races, but in the Toltec days, while two wives were allowed by the law, great numbers of men had only one wife. Nor were the women— as in countries nowadays where polygamy prevails— regarded as inferiors, or in the least oppressed. Their position was quite equal to that of the men, while the aptitude many of them displayed in acquiring the vril-power made them fully the equals if not the superiors of the other sex. This equality indeed was recognized from infancy, and there was no separation of the sexes in schools or colleges. Boys and girls were taught together. It was the rule, too, and not the exception, for complete harmony to prevail in the dual households, and the mothers taught their children to look equally to their father's wives for love and protection. Ñor were women debarred from taking part in the government. Sometimes they were members of the councils, and occasionally even were chosen by the Adept emperor to represent him in the various provinces as the local sovereigns.

The writing material of the Atlanteans consisted of thin sheets of metal, on the white porcelain-like surface of which the words were written. They also had the means of reproducing the written text by placing on the inscribed sheet another thin metal plate which had previously been dipped in some liquid. The text thus graven on the second plate could be reproduced at will on other sheets, a great number of which fastened together constituted a book.

A custom which differs considerably from our own must be instanced next, in their choice of food. It is an unpleasant subject but can scarcely be passed over. The flesh of the animals they usually discarded, while the parts which among us are avoided as food, were by then devoured. The blood also they drank— often hot from the animal— and various cooked dishes were also made of it.

It must not, however, be thought that they were without the lighter, and to us, more palatable, kinds of food. The seas and rivers provided them with fish, the flesh of which they ate, though often in such an advanced stage of decomposition as would be to us revolting. The different grains were largely cultivated, of which were made bread and cakes. They also had milk, fruit, and vegetables.

A small minority of the inhabitants, it is true, never adopted the revolting customs above referred to. This was the case with the Adept kings and emperors and the initiated priest* hood throughout the whole empire. They were entirely vegetarian in their habits, but though many of the emperor's counsellors and the officials about the court affected to prefer the purer diet, they often indulged in secret their grosser tastes.

Nor were strong drinks unknown in those days. Fermented liquor of a very potent sort was at one time much in vogue. But it was so apt to make these who drank it dangerously excited that a law was passed absolutely forbidding its consumption.

The weapons of warfare and the chase differed considerably at different epochs. Swords and spears, bows and arrows sufficed as a rule for the Rmoahals and the Tlavatli. The beasts which they hunted at that very early period were mam* moths with long woolly hair, elephants, and hippopotami. Marsupials also abounded as well as survivals of intermediate types— some being half reptile and half mammal, others half reptile and half bird.

The use of explosives was adopted at an early period and carried to great perfection in later times. Some appear to have been made to explode on concussion, others after a certain interval of time, but in either case, the destruction to life seems to have resulted from the release of some poisonous vapor, not from the impact of bullets. So powerful indeed must have become these explosives in later Atlantean times, that we hear of whole companies of men being destroyed in battle by the noxious gas generated by the explosion of one of these bombs above their heads, thrown there by some sort of lever.

The monetary system must now be considered. During the first three sub-races at all events, such a thing as a State coinage was unknown. Small pieces of metal or leather stamped with some given values were, it is true, used as tokens. Having a perforation in the center they were strung together and were usually carried at the girdle. But each man was as it were his own corner, and the leather or metal token fabricated by him and exchanged with another for value received, was but a personal acknowledgment of indebtedness, such as a promissory note is among us. No man was entitled to fabricate more of these tokens than he was able to redeem by the transfer of goods in his possession. The tokens did not circulate as coinage does, while the holder of the token had the means to estimate with perfect accuracy the resources of his debtor by the clairvoyant faculty which all then possessed to a greater or less degree, and which in any case of doubt was instantly directed to ascertain the actual state of the facts.

It must be stated, however, that in the later days of Poseidonis, a system approximating to our own currency was adopted, and the triple mountain visible from the great southern capital was the favorite representation on the State coinage.

But the system of land tenure is the most important subject under this heading. Among the Rmoahal and Tlavatli, who lived chiefly by hunting and fishing, the question naturally did not arise, though some system of village cultivation was recognized in the Tlavatli days.

It was with the increase of population and civilization in the early Toltec times that land first became worth fighting for. It is not proposed to trace the system or want of system prevalent in the troublous times anterior to the advent of the

Golden Age. But the records of that epoch present to the consideration, not only of political economists but of all who regard the welfare of the race, as a subject of the utmost interest and importance.

The population must be remembered had been steadily increasing, and under the government of the Adept emperors it had reached the very large figure already quoted; nevertheless, poverty and want were things undreamt of in those days, and this social well-being was no doubt partly due to the system of land tenure.

Not only was all the land and its produce regarded as belonging to the emperor, but all the flocks and herds upon it were his as well. The country was divided into different provinces or districts, each province having at its head one of the subsidiary kings or viceroys appointed by the emperor. Each of these viceroys was held responsible for the government and well-being of all the inhabitants under his rule. The tillage of the land, the harvesting of the crops, and the pasturage of the herds lay within his sphere of superintendence, as well as the conducting of stich agricultural experiments as have been already referred to.

Each viceroy had around him a council of agricultural advisers and coadjutors, who had amongst their other duties to be well versed in astronomy, for it was not a barren science in those days. The occult influences on plant and animal life were then studied and taken advantage of. The power, too, of producing rain at will was not uncommon then, while the effects of a glacial epoch were on more than one occasion partly neutralized in the northern parts of the continent by occult science. The right day for beginning every agricultural operation was of course duly calculated, and the work was carried into effect by the officials whose duty it was to supervise every detail.

The produce raised in each district or kingdom was as a rule consumed in it, but an exchange of agricultural commodities was sometimes arranged between the rulers.

After a small share had been put aside for the emperor and the central government at the "City of the Golden Gates," the produce of the whole district or kingdom was divided among6othe inhabitants— the local viceroy and bis retinue of officials naturally receiving the larger portions, but the meanest agricultural laborer getting enough to secure his competence and comfort. Any increase in the productive capacity of the land, or in the mineral wealth that it yielded, was divided proportionately amongst all concerned— all, therefore, were interested in making the result of their combined labor as lucrative as possible.

This system worked admirably for a very long period. But as time went on negligence and self-seeking crept in. Those whose duty it was to superintend, threw more and more responsibility on their inferiors in office, and in time it became rare for the rulers to interfere or to interest themselves in any of the operations. This was the beginning of the evil days. The members of the dominant class who had previously given all their time to the state duties began to think about making their own lives more pleasant. The elaboration of luxury was setting in.

There was one cause in particular that produced great dis- content amongst the lower classes. The system under which the youth of the nation was drafted into the technical schools has already been referred to. Now it was always one of the superior class whose psychic faculties had been duly cultivated, to whom the duty was assigned of selecting the children so that each one should receive the training, and ultimately be devoted to the occupation, for which he was naturally most fitted. But when those possessed of the clairvoyant vision, by which alone such choice could be made, delegated their duties to inferiors who were wanting in such psychic attributes, the results ensuing were that the children were often thrust into wrong grooves, and those whose capacity and taste lay in one direction often found themselves tied for life to an occupation which they disliked, and in which, therefore, they were rarely successful. The systems of land tenure which ensued in different parts of the empire on the breaking up of the great Toltec dynasty were many and various. But it is not necessary to follow them. In the later days of Poseidonis, they had, as a rule, given place to the system of individual ownership which we know so well.

Reference has already been made, under the head of "Emigrations," to the system of land tenure which prevailed during that glorious period of Peruvian history when the Incas held sway about 14,000 years ago. A short summary of this may be of interest as demonstrating the source from which its groundwork was doubtless derived, as well as instancing the variations which had been adopted in this somewhat more complicated system.

All title to land was derived in the first instance from the Inca, but half of it was assigned to the cultivators, who of course constituted the great bulk of the population. The other half was divided between the Inca and the priesthood who celebrated the worship of the sun.

Out of the proceeds of his specially allotted lands the Inca had to keep up the army, the roads throughout the whole empire, and all the machinery of government. This was con- ducted by a special governing class all more or less closely related to the Inca himself and representing a civilization and a culture much in advance of the great masses of the population.

The remaining fourth— "the lands of the sun"— provided not only for the priests who conducted the public worship throughout the empire, but for the entire education of the people in schools and colleges, for all sick and infirm persons, and finally, for every inhabitant (exclusive, of course, of the governing class for whom there was no cessation of work) on reaching the age of forty-five, that being the age arranged for the hard work of life to cease, and for leisure and enjoyment to begin.

Religion.—The only subject that now remains to be dealt with is the evolution of religious ideas.

Between the spiritual aspiration of a rude but simple race and the degraded ritual of an intellectually cultured but spiritually dead people, lies a gulf which only the term religion, used in its widest acceptation, can span. Nevertheless, it is this consecutive process of generation and degeneration which has to be traced in the history of the Atlantean people.

It will be remembered that the government under which the Rmoahals carne into existence, was described as the most perfect conceivable, for it was the Manu himself who acted as their king. The memory of this divine ruler was naturally preserved in the annals of the race, and in due time he carne to be regarded as a god, among a people who were naturally psychic and had consequently glimpses of those states of consciousness which transcend our ordinary waking condition. Retaining these higher attributes, it was only natural that these primitive people should adopt a religion, which, though in no way representative of any exalted philosophy, was of a type far from ignoble. In later days this phase of religious belief passed into a kind of ancestor worship.

The Tlavatli while inheriting the traditional reverence and worship for the Manu, were taught

The Story of Atlantis

by Adept instructors about the existence of a Supreme Being whose symbol was recognized as the sun. They thus developed a sort of sun worship, for the practice of which they repaired to the hilltops. There they built great circles of upright monoliths. These were intended to be symbolical of the sun's yearly course, but they were also used for astronomical purposes— being placed so that, to one standing at the high altar, the sun would rise at the winter solstice behind one of these monoliths, at the vernal equinox behind another, and so on throughout the year. Astronomical observations of a still more complex character connected with the more distant constellations were also helped by these stone circles.

We have already seen under the head of emigrations how a later sub-race— the Akkadians— in the erection of Stonehenge, reverted to this primitive building of monoliths.

Endowed though the Tlavatli were with somewhat greater capacity for intellectual development than the previous sub- race, their cult was still of a very primitive type.

With the wider diffusion of knowledge in the days of the Toltecs, and more especially with the establishment later on of an initiated priesthood and an Adept emperor, increased opportunities were offered to the people for the attainment of a truer conception of the divine. The few who were ready to take full advantage of the teaching offered, after having been tried and tested, were doubtless admitted into the ranks of the priesthood which then constituted an immense occult fraternity. With these, however, who had so outstripped the mass of humanity, as to be ready to begin the progress of the occult path, we are not here concerned, the religions practiced by the inhabitants of Atlantis generally being the subject of our investigation.

The power to rise to philosophic heights of thought was of course wanting to the masses of those days, as it is similarly wanting to the great majority of the inhabitants of the world today. The nearest approach that the most gifted teacher could make in attempting to convey any idea of the nameless and all-pervading essence of the Cosmos was necessarily imparted in the form of symbols, and the sun naturally enough was the first symbol adopted. As in our own days too, the more cultivated and spiritually minded would see through the symbol, and might sometimes rise on the wings of devotion to the Father of our spirits, that:

"Motive and center of our soul's desire, Object, and refuge of our journey's end"

while the grosser multitude would see nothing but the symbol and would worship it, as the carved Madonna or the wooden image of the crucified one is today worshipped throughout Catholic Europe.

Sun and tire worship then became the cult for the celebration of which magnificent temples were reared throughout the length and breadth of the continent of Atlantis, but more especially in the great "City of the Golden Gates"— the temple service being performed by retinues of priests endowed by the State for that purpose.

In those early days, no image of the Deity was permitted. The sun disk was considered the only appropriate emblem of the godhead, and as such was used in every temple, a golden disk being generally placed so as to catch the first rays of the rising sun at the vernal equinox or at the summer solstice.

An interesting example of the almost unalloyed survival of this worship of the sun disk may be instanced in the Shinto ceremonies of Japan. All other representation of Deity is in this faith regarded as impious, and even the circular mirror of polished metal is hidden from the vulgar gaze save on ceremonial occasions. Unlike the gorgeous temple decorations of Atlantis however, the Shinto temples are characterized by an entire absence of decoration— the exquisite finish of the plain woodwork being unrelieved by any carving, paint, or varnish.

But the sun -disk did not always remain the only permissible emblem of Deity. The image of a man— an archetypal man— was in after days placed in the temples and adored as the highest representation of the divine. In some ways this might be considered a reversion to the Rmoahal worship of the Manu. Even then the religion was comparatively pure, and the occult fraternity of the "Good Law" of course did their utmost to keep alive in the hearts of the people the spiritual life.

The evil days, however, were drawing near when no altruistic idea should remain to redeem the race from the abyss of selfishness in which it was destined to be overwhelmed. The decay of the ethical idea was the necessary prelude to the perversion of the spiritual. The hand of every man fought for himself alone, and his knowledge was used for purely selfish ends, till it became an established belief that there was nothing in the universe greater or higher than themselves. Each man was his own "Law, and Lord and God," and the very worship of the temples ceased to be the worship of any ideal but became the mere adoration of man as he was known and seen to be. As is written in the Book of Dzyan, "Then the Fourth became tall with pride. We are the kings it was they built huge said; we are the Gods cities. Of rare earths and metals, they built, and out of the fires vomited, out of the white stone of the mountains and of the black stone, they cut their own i m ages in their size and likeness and worshipped them." Shrines were placed in temples in which the statue of each man, wrought in gold or silver, or carved in stone or wood, was adored by himself. The richer men kept whole trains of priests in their employ for the cult and care of their shrines, and offerings were made to these statues as to gods. The apotheosis of self could go no further.

It must be remembered that every true religious idea that has ever entered into the mind of man, has been consciously suggested to him by the divine instructors or the Initiates of the Occult Lodges, who throughout all the ages Lave been the guardians of the divine mysteries, and of the facts of the supersensual states of consciousness.

Mankind generally has but slowly become capable of assimilating a few of these divine ideas, while the monstrous growths and hideous distortions to which every religion on earth stands as witness, must be traced to man's own lower nature. It would seem indeed that he has not always even been fit to be entrusted with knowledge as to the mere symbols under which were veiled the light of Deity, for in the days of the Turanian supremacy some of this knowledge was wrongfully divulged.

We have seen how the life and light giving attributes of the sun were in early times used as the symbol to bring before the minds of the people all that they were capable of conceiving of the great First Cause. But other symbols of far deeper and more real significance were known and guarded within the ranks of the priest hood. One of these was the conception of a Trinity in Unity. The Trinities of most sacred significance were never divulged to the people, but the Trinity personifying the cosmic powers of the universe as Creator, Preserver, and Destroyer, became publicly known in some irregular manner in the Turanian days. This idea was still further materialized and degraded by the Semites into a strictly anthropomorphic Trinity consisting of father, mother, and child.

A further and rather terrible development of the Turanian times must still be referred to. With the practice of sorcery many of the inhabitants had, of course, become aware of the existence of powerful elementals— creatures who had been called into being, or at least animated by their own powerful wills, which is directed towards maleficent ends, naturally produced the elementals of power and malignity. So degraded had then become man's feelings of reverence and worship, that they actually began to adore these semi-conscious creations of their own malignant thought. The ritual with which these beings were worshipped was blood-stained from the very start, and of course, every sacrifice offered at their shrine gave vitality and persistence to these vampire-like creations— so much so, that even to the present day in various parts of the world, the elementals formed by the powerful will of these old Atlantean sorcerers still continue to exact their tribute from unoffending village communities.

Though inaugurated and widely practiced by the brutal Turanians, this blood-stained ritual seems never to have spread to any extent among the other sub-races, though human sacrifices appear to have been not uncommon among some branches of the Semites.

In the great Toltec empire of Mexico, the sun-worship of their forefathers was still the national religion, while the bloodless offerings to their beneficent Deity, Quetzalcoatl, consisted merely of flowers and fruit. It was only with the coming of the savage Aztecs that the harmless Mexican ritual was supplemented with the blood of human sacrifices, which drenched the altars of their war god, Huitzilopochtli, and the tearing out of the hearts of the victims on the summit of the Teocalli may be regarded as a direct survival of the elemental-worship of their Turanian ancestors in Atlantis.

It will be seen then that as in our own days, the religious life of the people embraced the most varied forms of belief and worship. From the small minority who aspired to the initiation, and had touched with the higher spiritual life— who knew that goodwill towards all men, control of thought, and purity of life and action were the necessary preliminaries to the attainment of the highest states of consciousness and the widest realms of vision— innumerable phases led down through the more or less blind worship of cosmic powers, or of anthropo- morphic gods, to the degraded but most widely extended ritual in which each man adored his own image, and to the blood-stained rites of the

The Story of Atlantis

elemental worship.

It must be remembered throughout that we are dealing with the Atlantean race only, so that any reference would be out of place that bore on the still more degraded fetish-worship that even then existed— as it still does— amongst the debased representatives of the Lemurian peoples.

All through the centuries then the various rituals composed to celebrate these various forms of worship were carried on, till the final submergence of Poseidonis, by which time the countless hosts of Atlantean emigrants had already established on foreign lands the various cults of the mother continent.

To trace the rise and follow the progress in detail of the archaic religions, which in historic times have blossomed into such diverse and antagonistic forms, would be an undertaking of great difficulty, but the illumination it would throw on matters of transcendent importance may someday induce the attempt.

In conclusion, it would be vain to attempt to summarize what is already too much of a summary. Rather let us hope that the foregoing may lend itself as the text from which may be developed histories of the many offshoots of the various sub-races— histories that may analytically examine political and social developments which have been here touched on in the most fragmentary manner.

One word, however, may still be said about the evolution of the race— that progress which all creation, with mankind at its head, is ever destined to achieve century by century, millennium by millennium, manvantara by manvantara, and kalpa by kalpa.

The descent of spirit into matter— these two poles of the one eternal substance— is the process which occupies the first half of every eyelet. Now the period we have been contemplating in the foregoing pages— the period during which the Atlantean race was running its course— was the very middle or turning point of this present manvantara.

The process of evolution which in our present Fifth Race has now set in— the turn, that is, of matter into spirit— had in those days revealed itself in but a few isolated individual cases— forerunners of the resurrection of the spirit.

But the problem, which all who have given the subject any amount of consideration must have felt to be still awaiting a solution, is the surprising contrast in the attributes of the Atlantean race. Side by side with their brutal passions, their degraded animal propensities, were their psychic faculties, their godlike intuition.

Now the solution to this apparently insoluble enigma lies in the fact that the building of the bridge had only then begun— the bridge of Manas, or mind, destined to unite in the perfected individual the upward surging forces of the animal and the downward cycling spirit of the God. The animal kingdom of today exhibits a field of nature where the building of that bridge has not yet begun, and even among mankind in the days of Atlantis, the connection was so slight that the spiritual attributes had but little controlling power over the lower animal nature. The touch of mind they had was sufficient to add zest to the gratification of the senses but was not enough to vitalize the still dormant spiritual faculties, which in the perfected individual will have to become the absolute monarch. Our metaphor of the bridge may carry us a little further if we consider it as now in process of construction, but as destined to remain incomplete for mankind in general for untold millenniums— in fact, until Humanity has completed another circle of the seven planets and the great Fifth Round is halfway through its course.

Though it was during the latter half of the Third Root Race and the beginning of the Fourth that the Manasaputra[17] descended to endow with mind the bulk of Humanity who were still without the spark, yet so feebly burned the light all through the Atlantean days that few could be said to have attained to the powers of abstract thought. On the other hand, the functioning of the mind on concrete things carne well within their grasp, and as we have seen it was in the practical concerns of their everyday life, especially when their psychic faculties were directed towards the same objects, that they achieved such remarkable and stupendous results.

It must also be remembered that Kama, the fourth principle, naturally obtained its culminating

---

[17] Manasaputra is a Sanskrit title derived from two root words, viz. manasa and putra. 'Manasa' refers to the mind, and 'putra' means 'son', or 'progeny'. Manasaputra, therefore, may literally be translated as, 'mind-children' or the 'mind-born'. In Hinduism, the god Brahma is believed to have created sixteen sons and a daughter from his mind. This concept of creatio ex nihilo is also associated with the Vedic deity Prajapati, who has since been assimilated with Brahma. These children of the mind are stated to have been created or come into existence through the will of Brahma. The only manasaputri (mind-daughter) of Brahma is Saraswati, who was said to have been born from the mind of Brahma, though there are also texts that hold that she sprung from his tongue or his forehead. This is also the best indication that the mind-born are not genetically related to the creator, since Brahma is enraptured by Saraswati and goes on to choose her as his consort.

development in the Fourth Race. This would account for the depths of animal grossness to which they sank, whilst the approach of the cycle to its nadir inevitably accentuated this downward movement, so that there is little to be surprised at in the gradual loss by the race of the psychic faculties, and in its descent to selfishness and materialism.

Rather should all this be regarded as part of the great cyclic process in obedience to the eternal law.

We have all gone through those evil days, and the experiences we then accumulated go to make up the characters we now possess.

But a brighter sun now shines on the Aryan race than that which lit the path of their Atlantean forefathers. Less dominated by the passions of the senses, more open to the influence of the mind, the men of our race have obtained, and are obtaining, a firmer grasp of knowledge, and a wider range of intellect. This upward are of the great Manvantara cycle will naturally lead increasing numbers towards the entrance of the Occult Path, and will lend more and more attraction to the transcendent opportunities it offers for the continued strengthening and purification of the character—strengthening and purification no longer directed by mere spasmodic effort, and continually interrupted by misleading attractions, but guided and guarded at every step by the Masters of Wisdom, so that the upward climb when once begun should no longer be halting and uncertain, but lead directly to the glorious goal.

The psychic faculties too, and the godlike intuition, lost for lime but still the rightful heritage of the race, only await the individual effort of re-attainment, to give the character still deeper insight and more transcendent powers. So shall the ranks of the Adept instructors— the Masters of Wisdom— be ever strengthened and recruited, and even amongst us today there must certainly be some, indistinguishable save by the deathless enthusiasm with which they are animated, who will, before the next Root Race is established on this planet, stand themselves as Masters of Wisdom to help the race in its upward progress.

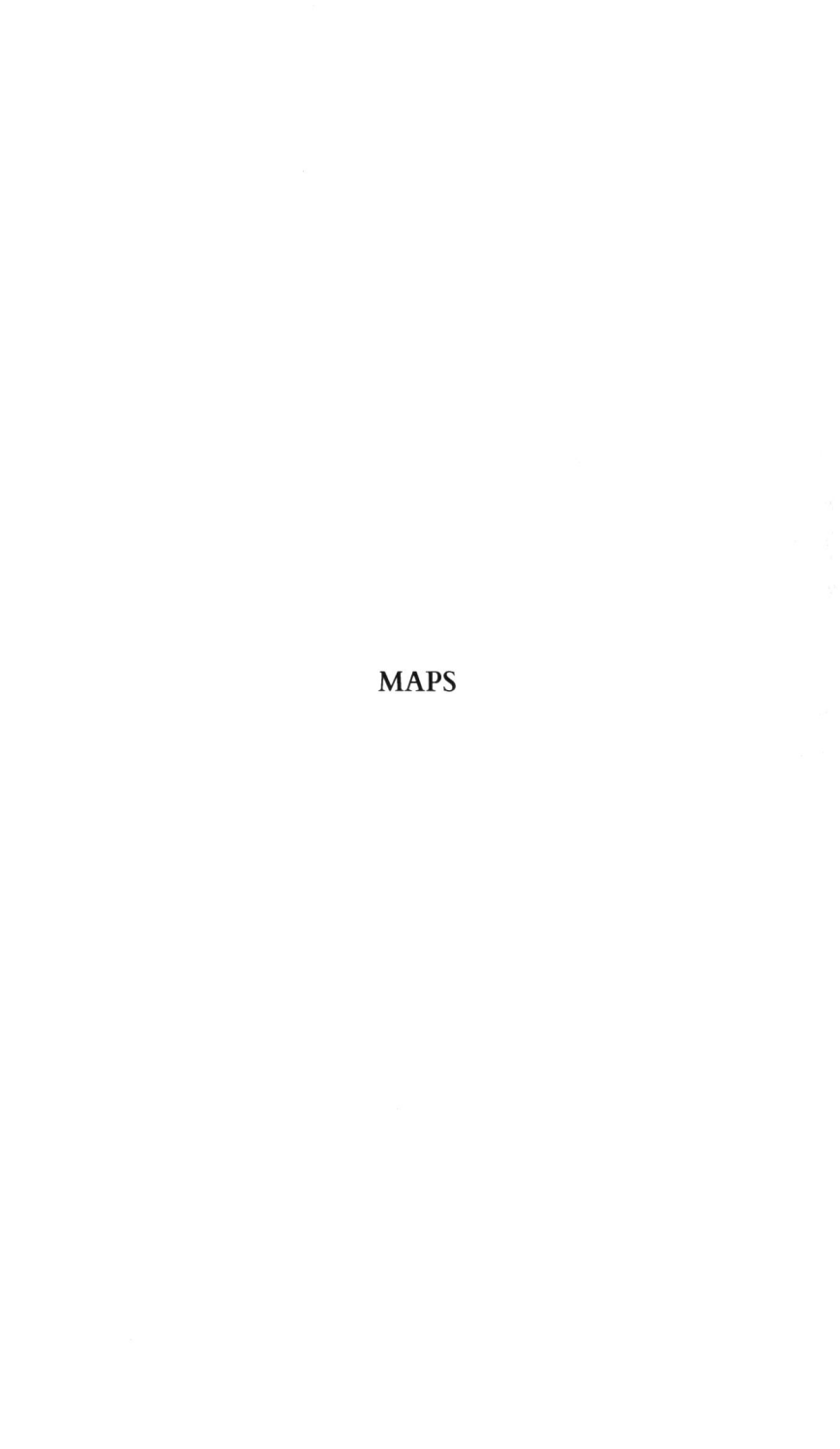

MAPS

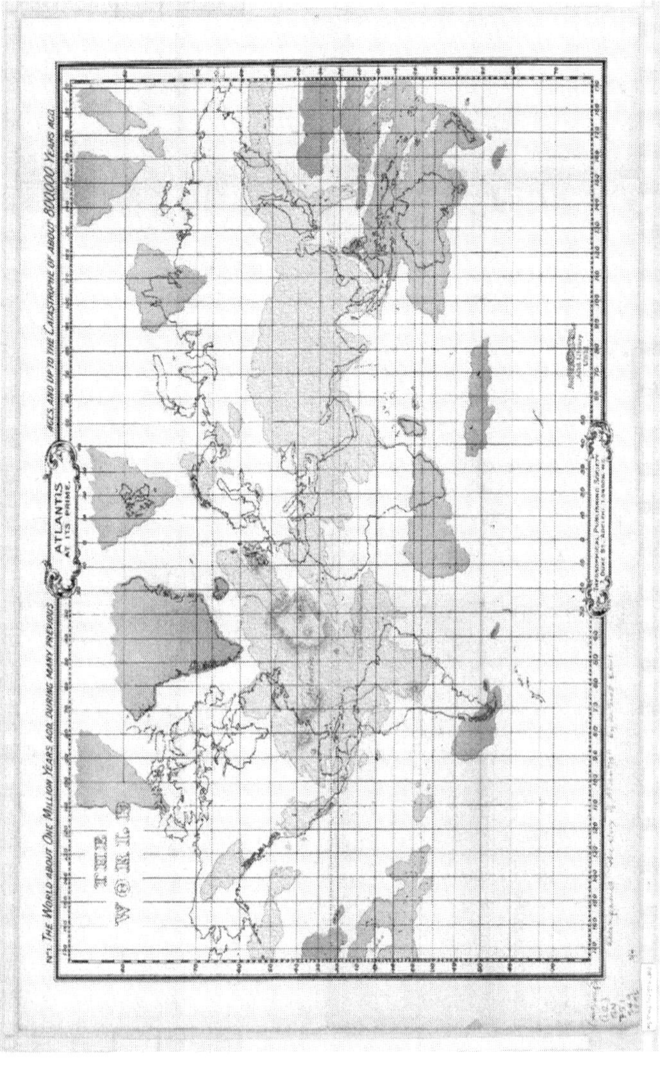
No. 1. THE WORLD ABOUT ONE MILLION YEARS AGO DURING MANY PREVIOUS AGES AND UP TO THE CATASTROPHE OF ABOUT 800,000 YEARS AGO
ATLANTIS AT ITS PRIME
THE WORLD

The Story of Atlantis

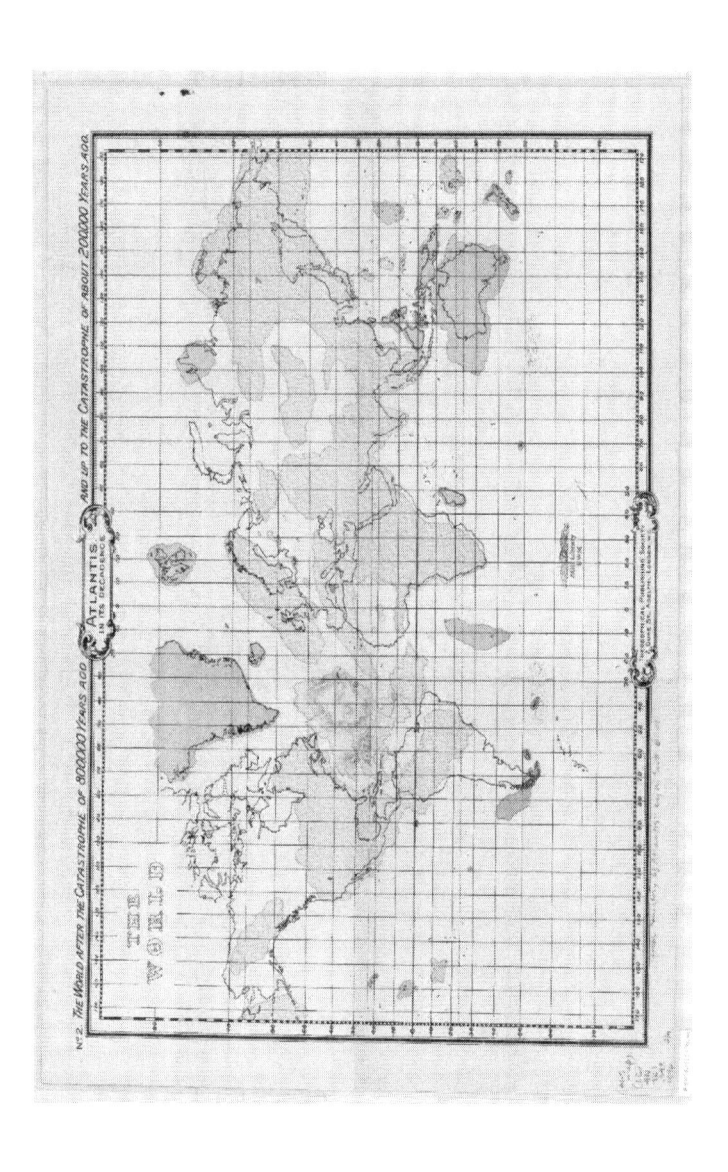

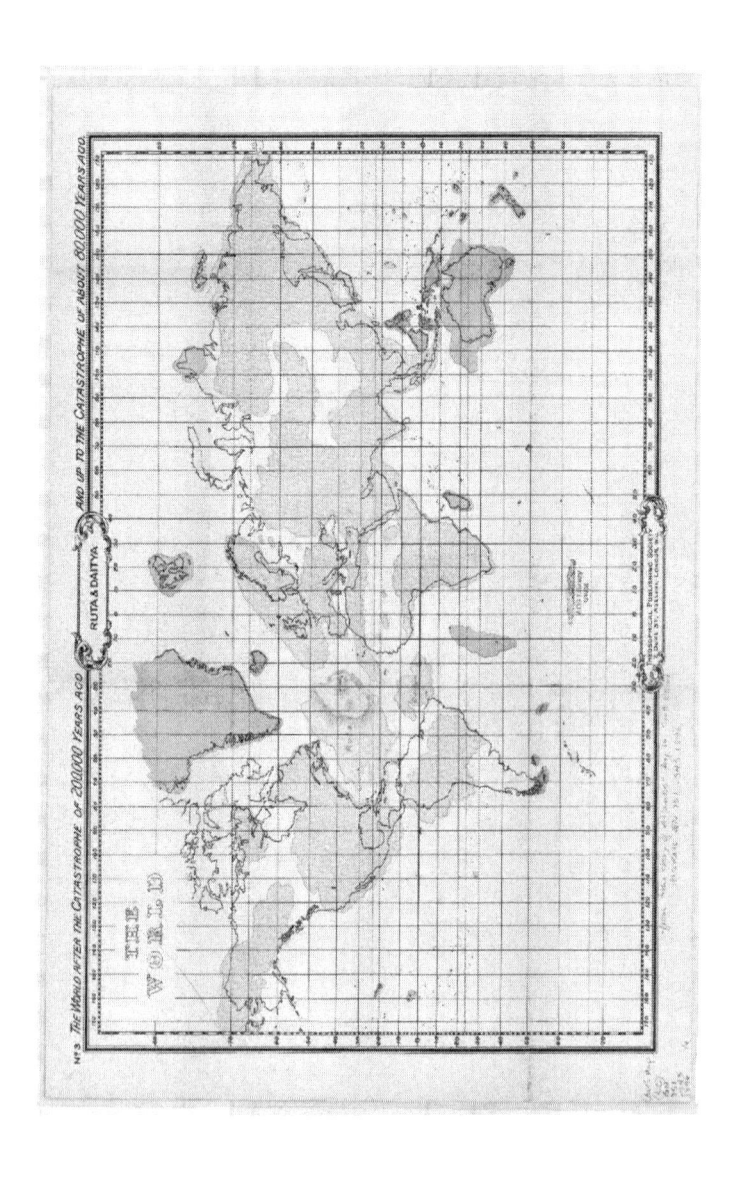

Nº 3. THE WORLD AFTER THE CATASTROPHE OF 200,000 YEARS AGO AND UP TO THE CATASTROPHE OF ABOUT 80,000 YEARS AGO

RUTA & DAITYA

The Story of Atlantis

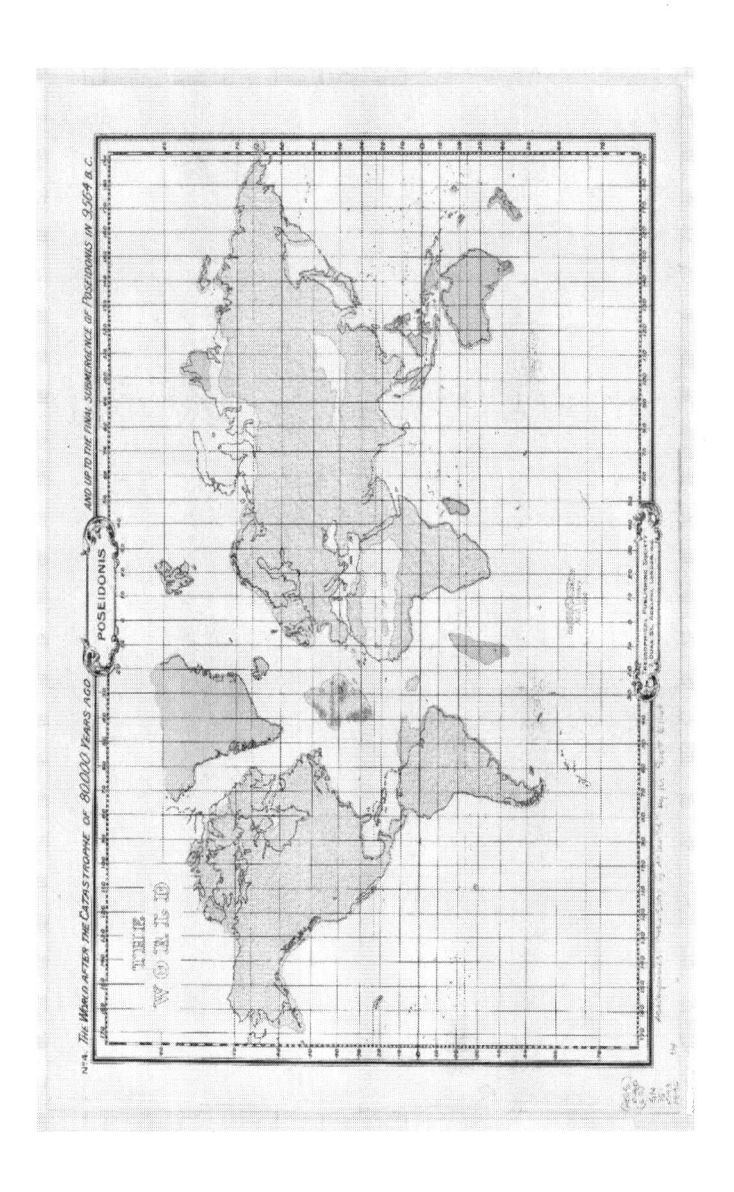